# JUDE

An elegy for Sarah Fishkin

A Play By

Lee Gundersheimer

For Jacob, Sarah, and the entire Fishkin families past and present. And for
Cassey Chou, who against her better judgement, understood.

For performance rights please contact the author at
lee.gunder@gmail.com.
In most cases, the rights will be waived as
an in kind donation to your theater.

# CAST OF CHARACTERS

A preferred ensemble of 18 performers. Can be larger or smaller depending on budgets and available performers. This is a play about community, so please err to the side of more performers if possible.

*Jacob*, an old Jewish man in his seventies, small in stature, but a huge heart

*Alan.*, a teacher of drama at NYU in his thirties or early forties, born Jewish but not a follower

*Sarah*, a young Polish Jew, ages from 13 to 18, much older than her years

*Jakov*, Jacob as a young boy, a fireball, ages from 11- 19

*Shoshka*, Jacob and Sarah's mother, in her late thirties early forties, a former political activist

*David*, Jacob and Sarah's father, late thirties, early forties, a shoemaker, photographer, farmer- jack of all trades

*Mere Lebbe*, their youngest daughter, six

*Yitzhok*, their youngest son, seven

*Deb*, Alan's good friend, a performance artist and fellow Jew

*Kate*, Alan's wife, not Jewish, an immigrant from another country

*Actress 1,* (in her sixties) plays Bobie, Stozipicrow, and Rabbi's Wife

*Actress 2,* (in her fifties) plays Magda, Dantcheka, and Rohkol

*Student 1*, also plays Policeman, Soldier, Motyl, short Partisan

*Student 2*, also plays Doctor, Yerek, Leyzer

*Student 3*, also plays Fanya, Kahne

*Actor 1,* plays Mr. Eisenbaud, Publisher, Moses, Getzel, Yerek's Father, Reb Moishe, and Mr. Schulz

*Actor 2,* plays Tall Partisan, Speaker, Reb Chaim, and Arieh

*Actor 3,* (in his fifties) Partisan Leader, Rabbi, Stozipioz, German Commander, Ronthsk

### *ACT ONE*

*The stage has many different areas that will be used. Furniture and set pieces should be kept to a minimum and place should be delineated primarily with lighting and/or projections. Often the action will take place in many different times and places simultaneously, a fugue.*

*In single spots we will hear a disjointed chorus of voices but the first sight we see is of an old man lying on his back in his undershirt and some boxer shorts. It is not clear whether he is alive or dead. His eyes are closed. If possible it is raining on him. Finally he speaks:*

JACOB.. Am I lost…

*And now the voices, one tumbling upon the next, sometimes difficult to distinguish between them or possibly they overlap, music is helpful underneath and will be throughout the play:*

VOICE 1 (SARAH.). Do I live or am I already dead…

VOICE TWO. I have trouble sleeping…

VOICE THREE. This is real life…

VOICE FOUR. This is somebody's real life this time

VOICE FIVE. How do you make sense of that? The randomness?

VOICE SIX. How dare they say I am going to die!

VOICE SEVEN. I am nowhere through living!

VOICE EIGHT. I feel I am speaking to the future.

VOICE NINE. They will never be able to take away our memories.

VOICE TEN. How rich was the content of last night's dream

*The voices continue distributed however it seems fit:*

How angry I am at myself and my imagination.

One must make peace with one's fate

Bad times,

Hunger

And death,
Await us

A symphony is being written just for us

One must go on living

To see true happiness one day

There is always time

My story is Sarah's story

As is yours

Here is the first volume of the catalogue of Eastern European mid-twentieth century material

Our battle is with time

A collection is when we have a substantial group

Each year counts

Each collection has its own box

The difference between five or ten or a hundred

We measure these things in stages

That is quite a victory is it not?

> *The old man stands and puts on a pair of checked shorts and a loose button front shirt like they wear in the tropics.*

Each stage is significant

*He puts on some tall stretch socks and some old khaki loafers.*

You cannot transcend what you do not acknowledge

What is the dimension of such a sacrifice?

Life and courage are your gifts

Where was I?

Sometimes I forget…

But that is another story

How do you make sense of that?

The randomness?

I am being tested here

And I have to make the most of it

In the pounding of your pulse

I hear your screaming

I hear hell

You must let go

Do you know I used to escape?

But that is another story

I've tasted no joy in reality

In dreams let my spirit run free

What can life be like

Look at the whole picture

When my soul is taken from me

Don't worry I watch over you.

Look into the faces

And past the faces

Hold onto that ache

There?  Do you see?

Because it means that you are still alive

> *The voices are lit just enough to see they are carrying ladders of varying lengths. These ladders will become most of the set pieces. For now they become door frames and some become a desk and a chair.*

Now you will live to paint again

And you will paint more beautiful and splendid pictures

Am I alive now?

Yes, I am writing

By thy will

And Thy leave

All of us may go on living

> *The old man is now standing outside of an office area at New York University's Department of Drama. The time is 2001. He does not seem to know where to go.*

JACOB. I must be lost…

*He chooses an office from the many doorframes and knocks.*

ALAN. Can I help you- *(Phone rings and will quite often)* Hang on- Hello this is Alan- hey-hang on a second- Yes?

JACOB. I wonder if you are the one who can help me?

ALAN.. Yes *(phone rings again)* Hang on- Hello, this is Alan- can you hold please? Deb, can I get back to you in a minute? Thanks. I'm sorry, now what is it?

JACOB. If this time is bad I could come back later?

ALAN. I am a little swamped right now, yes, *(The phone rings again)* Excuse me- but- did we have an appointment?

JACOB. No. They sent me to you. They said you are the one who would help.

ALAN. Did they. And what exactly is it that I will help you with?

JACOB. I have a diary-

ALAN. *(Phone is still ringing-)* I'm sorry, did you say diary?

*From another area we hear a young girl screaming a name:*

SARAH. Jakov!!!

JACOB. Yes, my sister-

ALAN. Hang on- This is ALAN.- Oh, hey sweetheart, are you feeling better? No?

SARAH. Jakov!!! Jakov!!!

ALAN. You at work?

JAKOV. *(A young boy, 12, playing. Both realities overlapping)* What- what! I'm studying!

ALAN. *(To JACOB.)* A diary- you say?

SARAH. Did you touch my diary? You did, didn't you!

JACOB. Yes- from the war.

JAKOV. No, I did not touch your precious diary. Your solid gold diary. It is forbodden. Thou shalt not touch Sarah's diary…

ALAN. *(To the phone call.)* Can I call you right back. Sorry- *(They have hung up.)*

SARAH. Do not go telling lies, and do not make fun of the Lord's commandments. And do not touch my diary!

JACOB. You must forgive me. I do not mean to intrude.

JAKOV. I could care less about your stupid diary! I could care less if you spend all day writing in that stupid book. When other girls are out playing or sewing or helping their mothers, I could care less that you would rather write and write….

SARAH. Someday you'll understand. You're just a boy-

JAKOV. I'm not a boy. I'm eleven, almost twelve, and I've been to the forest with Betar, and I've eaten berries and lived for days and can start a fire by myself- and I run faster than anyone for miles- and you, all you do is sit and scribble.

ALAN. You say you have a diary?

JACOB. Yes.

ALAN. And you want my help?

JACOB. Yes. They said you put on plays. That you might be able to help me to tell the story-

JAKOV. Who cares!  No one reads it but you. So who even knows what it says. Or if it says anything at all…

ALAN. And this diary is yours?

JACOB. No, it was my sister's. Sarah.. Sarah Fishkin. She died. When they liquidated our ghetto…

JAKOV. Why write a stupid diary if no one but you ever reads it?

ALAN. Please, sit down. I don't know what I can do. But please, have a seat.

JACOB. Thank you. My name is Jacob. Jacob Fishkin.

ALAN. Alan. Alan Klutzenburg.

JACOB. Klutzenburg?

ALAN. Yes, blame my father. It's German. German Jewish.

SARAH. Jakov, my sweet silly little brother, the diary is not for me or for you. It is for those who will come long after you and I…

ALAN. Not many of us left, I know…I'm so sorry… Forgive me-

JACOB. Please. No need. We were from Poland…My family. Near Minsk in a little shtetl called Rubzewitz. And my sister and my brothers and my whole family perished. I was the only one who survived- but my sister's diary was found-

SARAH. If - if something should happen- we will still have my diary-

JACOB. This was a miracle you see-

JAKOV. What would happen? What do you mean? Why do you talk so?

JACOB. The diary – it was intact- just as she said it would be-

JAKOV. Mother! Mother! Sarah is scaring me. She is saying that bad things will happen! Go away! Go!

ALAN. Wait- this was a diary you said-

JACOB. Yes, but my sister put on plays you see. She loved plays. "Yakov," she'd say-

JACOB and SARAH. "in a play, peasants can be prophets."

SARAH. I have visited Jerusalem, and I have seen Solomon's Temple!

JAKOV. You are crazy…When?

SARAH. Just last month. You will see little brother. Be in our play and you will no longer be just Jakov…

JACOB. And this came to me one day. Her story must be a play.  People love plays, no?

ALAN. Those that see them. Let's face it. On the used-to-be-vital-but-no-longer-essential-to-humanity list we are one notch above poets but two below clowns.

JACOB. And this is why you have this department for drama, no? And all these students who dream of acting? Because no one wants to see? I think not. Sarah would have loved it here…*(He stops a moment and sighs.)* So her diary will be a play.

> *Some students appear in an area and as one speaks, Alan turns and talks with them.*

STUDENT. A play about a young Jewish girl who wrote a diary- and died in World War II?

ALAN. Yes-

ANOTHER STUDENT. Hate to tell you Alan, but it's been done.

ALAN. I know, and so does he.

JACOB. I know what you are thinking- Anna Frank-

ALAN. He was selling me. Like some poor writer in Hollywood. Pitching his sister Sarah's story.

JACOB. But Sarah is different. Sarah was not in hiding. She was in the middle of a ghetto, and she was a journalist. She wanted to be a writer- her writing- she is not just a little girl. She wrote essays on the future of the Jewish people. She was a scholar-

ENSEMBLE.  **Lecture No. 10 Thursday, December 15, 1938 Kislev. Back To The Forgotten Jewish Ideas**

> *Throughout the play the ensemble will announce diary headings and perhaps projections are used. Sarah is seen in a pool of light reciting; each time she speaks alone the passages are directly from a translation of her actual diary:*

*SARAH.* Each individual has his own feelings, his thoughts and his faith in his beliefs. There are all sorts of peoples in the world. There are nations that have no idea; there are others that do have an idea, a religion. We are an idea that has a nation. That is how Jews have always understood their fate. We are the creation of an idea. Our life, our hearts are enchanted by its magic. By some sort of miracle our forefathers ignited a flame in our hearts that can never be extinguished. Moses' bush remains a permanent glowing in our blood. No one has the power to put it out.

ALAN. *(Turning back to JACOB.)* She was an old soul-

JACOB. Yes- you understand- this is a thirteen year old- her writing- it is like a rabbi- *(He takes out a very thick Xerox manuscript)* Here, I want you to read. We have over six years- two years before the war and four years during – *(He takes out another large manuscript)* and my memoirs…

ALAN. *(Turning back to the students)* He's been trying for years, you know.

STUDENT. I'll bet he has.

ALAN. I know it's crazy, but there is something about him-

STUDENT. Who needs another Holocaust play- with all due respect? I mean, what could you possibly say-

ANOTHER STUDENT. Been there, done that-

PUBLISHER. *(appears in another area)* Look, Mr. Fishking, I'm as Jewish as any other publisher in town, but forgive me- your sister- she says some very upsetting things. She actually forsakes God. "Where indeed is our Father? How could one who is merciful towards all living things be witness to all this and be silent? Am I the first to disapprove and to say there is no heavenly one?" We cannot be a part of publishing this.

ANOTHER STUDENT. Wait. Let me get this straight. She gets pissed at God?

ALAN. Yes. For one day. One day in six years, in the middle of a holocaust, she gets a little angry-

PUBLISHER. She denounces God. No one will publish a diary that says such things.

STUDENT. Wait a minute! They think that is wrong? It's so human for Christ's sake-

ANOTHER STUDENT. "My god why has thou forsaken me...."

ALAN. Exactly. She is very insightful but also full of rage and fear-

SARAH. *(From the diary)* Yes, it may well be that right now my pen is not referring to Thee in the proper fashion, but my patience has exploded and today I must write the truth about my dominant thoughts. It is probable that six years ago I would not have said this nor written in this manner, but now, as I observe the suffering of the Jewish people, see the nation drowning in a cruel sea of trouble without anyone coming to the rescue- no, just the opposite is taking place: the oppressors are being helped to touch bottom— as we drown, I am impelled to write. I see no help underway; there is silence everywhere. All else lives; we are alone in travail.

JACOB. Believe me, for Sarah to write such things- it is only because she was so devoted to the Lord. Rabbis used to love when Sarah visited. She couldn't wait to talk with them and they to her. This was a very exceptional student of Torah-

PUBLISHER. No student of Torah turns her back on God!

SARAH. Hasn't the path to righteousness with its guideposts marked Humanity, Unity, Fraternity, and Love been blocked off? In actuality been replaced by just the opposite? In place of brotherhood we see signs of divisiveness, alienation, separation. Instead of unity and love, we see brutality, barbarism, crudeness. If such repulsive behavior is encompassing the entire world, if only the few enjoy the full cup of happiness, while the greater number, ninety-nine percent, are thirsty, this can no longer continue.

STUDENT. Wow! Some girl fifty years ago wrote that? I said that to you just like yesterday about Bosnia-

ANOTHER STUDENT. Dude, when are you starting this?

ALAN. Tomorrow. Some of us are meeting to piece the story out.

ANOTHER STUDENT. We'll be there.

STUDENT. I'm down. Cause I always wondered why Anne Frank just never threw a hissy fit.

ANOTHER STUDENT. Yo, she did - at her sister and mother, and that fat woman in the attic.

STUDENT. Yeah, but not at the world- or at God. You read your Old Testament lately? I mean Yahweh was fierce.

> *Loud thunder and rain is heard. Lights shift to an assembly area in Rubzewitz, Poland, 1938.*

JAKOV. Ahhh!

SARAH. Jakov!

JAKOV. What!

SARAH. Where are you going?

JAKOV. I hate the thunder.

SARAH. No need to be scared…

JAKOV. I am not scared! *Another thunder clap.* No one will even be here. Let's just go home.

SARAH. Of course they will. All of us are ready. We rehearsed yesterday most of the day.

JAKOV. Yes. Instead of working.

SARAH. Our play is work too, little complainer… to tell the story of Joseph to all the shtetl is as important a job as working in the field. We must be reminded that others before us suffered-

JAKOV. But we know the story, we even know the end. This is what is so stupid about plays- everyone knows we are just acting, and they know the end-

SARAH. If you know a song- does that mean you shouldn't sing it?

JAKOV. Who is there to sing to? No one! It is pouring down rain. There will be no one here. Look at that sky- we are the only fools silly enough to come out in this weather.

> *The lights also come up on a rehearsal room at NYU. Actors are seen sitting waiting to hear Alan speak. The same actors play the "actors" in Sarah's play waiting for their audience to arrive.*

ALAN. Thank you all for coming, thank you. Especially in this weather. But it couldn't be more perfect. Because the first scene-the first scene in the play we are here to create takes place in the middle of a storm *(The thunder is heard again)* It was pouring down rain. And the Fishkin family was going to a play. Sarah was part of a young girl's Jewish leadership group, and she persuaded them to put on a play. She created the whole thing. She wrote it and produced it. About the story of Joseph.

ANOTHER STUDENT. Yo, like Joseph and the Amazing Technicolor Dreamcoat-

STUDENT 3. I played the Pharaoh last summer in Maine.

ALAN. But what is so cool is this was very radical. These girls you see, got together to tell this story about all these sons. Dressed up like a bunch of men-

ANOTHER STUDENT. There goes our NEA grant...

JAKOV. You look ridiculous anyway. Dressed up like that. You all do.

FANYA. What about you, little sheep…

JAKOV. I am not a sheep, Fanya. I am a goat. And I get sacrificed so they can use my blood to claim Joseph was murdered. So I am a very important goat-

14

ANOTHER STUDENT. That's right, they faked Joseph's murder, smeared his coat with blood-

STUDENT. That is sooo "Silence of the Lambs"….

ALAN. And the girls had prepared for weeks and were all ready to perform.

FANYA. Little goat, get into place.

SARAH. We want to begin as soon as everyone gets here.

JAKOV. It's been an hour and half.  This goat is going home!

*Loud thunder. The sound of children screaming.*

SOSHKA. Sarah? Sarah?

SARAH. Mamma, thank you for coming.

SOSHKA. Thank you? Of course you don't need to thank. But why today? Why in this weather? We had to wait under a tree until we could continue-

SARAH. Here, dry yourself off.

SOSHKA. Why are you wearing such a silly coat? Look at you.  What happened to your hair?

SARAH. It is under the turban, Mother. I am one of the sons. Later on, I play the Pharaoh.

BOBIE. Some Pharaoh!  You look like my Uncle Simon… More hair on my elbow, than on Simon.

SARAH. Bobie, sit down. You walked all this way.

BOBIE. What you think I can't walk? I walk every day. Who gets the water if I can't walk?

DAVID. Sit down and rest mammala. We have forty days and forty nights this story takes.

SARAH. That's the flood, Pappa. That was last year's play.

DAVID. Oh, I thought with the rain and Jakov dressed like a monkey-

JAKOV. I'm a goat! An important goat! I am sacrificed!

DAVID. Oh, Abraham is it. Forgive me. You should do Noah with all this rain…

SARAH. It is Joseph-

DAVID. But you said goat-

JAKOV. There is a goat in this one too.

SARAH. And this is what we rehearsed, Pappa. You can't just change because of the weather.

MERRE LIEBE. Look at Jakov!

YITZKOHK. Look, a chicken!

SHOSHKE. Merre Liebe, Yitzhok. Sit down.

YITZKOHK.I want to play with the chicken.

JAKOV. Baaa- Baaaa! Does a chicken go Baaa?

SHOSHKE. He's a sheep, darlings-

JAKOV. A goat!

SHOSHKE. Well, a sheep goes baaa-

JAKOV. But I am a goat! They rub Joseph's coat in goat's blood, not a sheep! They are going to slit my throat!

BOTH CHILDREN. Mamma, Mamma!-

SHOSHKE. Children, sit down. Jakov, you are scaring them!

DAVID. They want to begin.

JAKOV. But there is no one here.

BOBIE. We are here!

SARAH. But the whole shtetl? Rohkol? And Fanya's family? Did you not see any others?

SHOSHKE. I don't know. There was so much rain.

BOBIE. Well - WE ARE HERE!

DAVID. Yes!

BOBIE. And I didn't walk all this way just to wash my schmarta in the rain!

SARAH. All right everybody, let's go from the beginning!

> *The actors all go into place and begin their play which will actually become the next scene in the woods.*

SARAH. Now, we think times are difficult for us now…

ALAN. So they performed the play?

JACOB. Yes. They performed for just a handful of people.

ALAN. How sad.

JACOB. Not at all. Sarah was very proud. See you have to understand my sister Sarah. She was like a rare stone. If most do a thing this way- Sarah would do it that way. And she loved being a Jew. For example, she wanted to go and study with a famous Zionist teacher. Travel to another shtetl, and study what was in store for the Jewish people. She was so interested in the future of our people. *(He stops for a brief moment overcome by the irony of that statement.)*

ALAN. Here, would you like some water.

JACOB. Yes, thank you. Very kind. Well, all right, normally this would be nothing special. But you see, the war, it was almost starting. And the Russians they were already occupying. And the Germans were already killing…And in the middle of this, she wanted to go at least forty kilometers away to build for a brighter future. So she went away, and things became even worse. You must understand the gentile farmers- they could get some salt and some flour for turning in a Jew. Oh yes. And they would. We tried to get them to help us- the farmers who knew us, were our friends- to send a wagon to go and get her. But even the most sympathetic begged us not to ask. It could mean deportation or death. Understandable, no? I ask you, would you help? To do this for a friend, if it might mean your death, would you go?

ENSEMBLE. **Sunday, 22nd June 1941, Wolozin. Today the War Between the Russians and the Germans Began.**

SARAH. Last night I slept so restfully, dreaming dreams of beautiful fantasy, a true balm to my unconscious. How rich was the content of last night's dream. If only it could last on and on. How disappointing to wake up and realize it was all a utopian vision. How angry I am at myself and my imagination. And now it is three o'clock. I couldn't possibly have imagined that upon going into the street I would hear such startling reports. Several seconds earlier I certainly had no idea that a war had broken out.

STUDENT. Yo, what's up?

ANOTHER STUDENT. A plane flew into the World Trade Center.

STUDENT. That's not funny.

ANOTHER STUDENT. I'm serious. Turn on the news. *(They hold up a remote and turn on a TV.)*

STUDENT. I thought you were like telling a joke. So this plane flies into the World Trade Center…

ANOTHER STUDENT. No, a couple of minutes ago.

STUDENT. My God, look at that- it's like flying right into the goddamn building-

ANOTHER STUDENT. That's not it. That's another one-

STUDENT. No, look it's flying right into the building. Just like you said.

ANOTHER STUDENT. I'm telling you it already happened.

STUDENT. It's a replay-

ANOTHER STUDENT. No, it's not. Look the other building is already smoking; that's the other tower-that's another plane!

STUDENT. Holy shit!!!

ENSEMBLE. **Monday, 23rd June 1941 (Wolozin)**

SARAH. It was with altered conceptions and very different emotions that everyone sets out for work today. Our thoughts are now dominated by questions of all sorts. We are all now thinking of the moments soon to come. One must make peace with one's fate. These times are very strained. Mobilization has begun. There is great hustle-bustle. One feels so helpless,

18

so lacking in personal effectiveness. Each one asks himself how will it all turn out. Sometimes the answer is tragic. Bad times—hunger and death await us.

SOSHKA. We must go for Sarah.

DAVID. Shoshka…

SOSHKA. I'll go to Wolozin on foot. If no one will help us. I will find a way. I will bring my daughter home.

DAVID. Have you walked to Wolozin? Through the woods? You will get lost!

JAKOV. Taté! Let Sarah stay where she is. She will only fight with us if she comes home.

JACOB. Now, my father was a gentle man, you see, but he had a tone of voice, never loud, never stern. But when he used that tone of voice- there was no use arguing.

DAVID. I will go.

JACOB. This was no easy task. Forty kilometers walking, but he knew the terrain. My father did many odd jobs for the farmers- worked with animals, when they were sick. He made them shoes. For the farmers, not the animals…

ALAN. He made shoes.

JACOB. Oh, yes, the best. Everyone loved my father's shoes. He even taught me how to make them. And it was a good thing, but this is another story… He'd taste the soil and predict the harvest and cut hair –oh, and he was a photographer. Whenever there was a death, Father was called upon to photograph the deceased. It had become a custom to postpone the burial until after photos were taken. And he would take pictures at weddings… My Taté was a very well known man throughout the area-

JAKOV. I have a good idea, Taté! I will go with you.

DAVID and SHOSKA. You?

JACOB. They both said it at the same time. And I remember I just had to laugh.

JAKOV. Of course. I love the woods. I love to watch the birds fly from branch to branch and the way the forest smells. I've been to the woods with Betar. I can start a fire without using matches.

YITZKOHK. Yes, yes, I want to go, too.

MERRE LIEBE. Go where?

YITZKOHK. To the woods with Jakov and Pappa.

MERRE LIEBE. I want to go!

SHOSKA. This is not Betar, Jakov!

DAVID. This danger is very real.

JAKOV. I can run fast. If there is danger I can run for help!!! I don't care what it is. Death, schmeth!

JACOB. And I remember that night I was so excited I couldn't sleep. I knew I was doing something so important!

STUDENT. It's bull-crap. It all seems like- so petty. Put on a play? In the middle of this chaos? We are supposed to rehearse a play…?

ANOTHER STUDENT. No way. I mean what difference could this possible make.

YET ANOTHER STUDENT. We may all die tomorrow…All of a sudden it makes theater- it makes being an artist look pretty fucking unimportant.

STUDENT. I'm volunteering to help downtown, gonna do something productive!

ANOTHER STUDENT. I tried that. They have too many people. They turn you away.

YET ANOTHER STUDENT. Most of us can't even get anywhere. There are no trains past 14th street.

ALAN. You can walk-

STUDENT. I know. Yesterday we had to walk home. All the way uptown.

ALAN. And yet you came to rehearse, why?

ANOTHER STUDENT. Because I can't stand sitting at home and waiting…

YET ANOTHER STUDENT. Glued to the tube watching CNN… Like some zombie.

STUDENT. Broadway was deserted. It was really creepy…

ANOTHER STUDENT. People had to walk across the bridge to Brooklyn. There are no trains and cars, so everyone is just walking across the bridges. Sort of stone-faced and quiet.

SHOSHKA. Get up and get dressed you two. Don't waste any time. You need the dark. Here, take this food I prepared for you.

ENSEMBLE. **Wednesday, 25th June 1941, Wolozin. Today the Germans Entered Our City and Captured It.**

DAVID. No, keep this. We have so little. I know plenty of peasants on the way, and they know me. We won't go hungry.

SARAH. *(In another light.)* We were afraid to remain indoors any longer and went out to an orchard, where we waited calmly for Death to approach. It is terrible when bullets are flying overhead, and it seems that at any moment one of them will strike and put an end to our young lives. But how wonderfully the heart, filled with absolute calm, dictates: With much confidence we continue to look Death right in the eye and wait to see what will happen in the hours immediately ahead. I feel in my quaking heart the desire to perish together with my family, to end my young life beside my parents.

JAKOV. Mother, you remind me of the story of Abraham and Isaac. Abraham woke his son and took him to the altar to be sacrificed. But an angel came down from Heaven and spared Isaac's life. Nothing will happen to us. Angels will watch over us.

SHOSKA. God be with you.

JAKOV. You see Taté, Mamma is a strong woman. She isn't crying.

SHOSKA. Go now, hurry. Soon it will be too light

JACOB. It must have been agony for her. Who knew if we'd ever come back. You could hear the sounds of the German trucks. On every road. So we went further and further into the woods. After what seemed like five forevers, it was the middle of the day and yet it was almost pitch black, the trees were so thick. And my legs felt like iron weights.

DAVID. Do you hear that noise?

JAKOV. Yes.

DAVID. Those are more trucks. But the Germans will not enter the woods because it is not safe for them. They are afraid of the Partisans. We can rest a moment here.

JACOB. Like your American cowboys we used to play Partisan when we were little boys. There were stories of how brave they were, and we all wanted to fight the Germans like them.

JAKOV. *(He curls up in his Father's arms, trying to fight off sleep, but losing the battle)* I'm not afraid of the Partisans. I want to play with their rifles. I hear they all carry big rifles and can shoot like this- pop! Pop!

DAVID. Jakov. No! Keep your voice down.

JAKOV. Sorry. Sorry. *(Yawns)* Taté, when I was in Kheder I learned that the Jews wandered in the wilderness of Sinai for forty years. That is a long time, isn't it?

DAVID. Yes. It is.

JAKOV. My feet are so sore; I think I know how they felt.

DAVID. Oh, no little one. This is very different. Look at all these trees. There were no trees in the desert. And it was so very hot…

JAKOV. *(He is almost asleep now.)* Yes, but those Jews wanted to get home, too.

DAVID. And God brought them safely there.

JAKOV. And God is the same. He hasn't changed, so don't worry. We won't get lost, and we will come home safely. Because God brought them home.

DAVID. Yes, all but one.

JAKOV. All but one…?

DAVID. Yes…didn't they teach you in Kheder? Moses…. *(He sees the boy is asleep and so he, too, rests his eyes.)*

JACOB. Now, when we sat down to rest, it was the middle of the day. But we must have been exhausted because now it was dark and we were still sound asleep.

*Two men are seen creeping up on the sleeping father and son.*

FIRST MAN. Don't move or we will shoot!

SECOND MAN. Not a word!

JAKOV. *(Sees them before his Father and surprisingly doesn't not scream.)* Are you a real Partisan? I know how to survive in the woods, too! You are a real Partisan- and you have a rifle too.

SHORT PARTISAN. I said be quiet!

DAVID. *(Waking)* JAKOV.?

TALL PARTISAN. Don't move.

JAKOV. This is my Taté, my father. We are on our way to Wolozin to pick up our sister-

SHORT PARTISAN. And I am on the way to Paris. Be quiet!

DAVID. Jakov! The nice men want us to be quiet.

TALL PARTISAN. What language do you speak?

JAKOV. How can I answer you and not speak at the same time?

DAVID. Russian -

JAKOV. And Yiddish!  And I know Hebrew! I studied in Kheder!

DAVID. Jakov, do what the nice men ask.

JAKOV. But you just talked!

ALAN. No! So you basically just told them you were Jews.

JACOB. Yes, but I thought they were Partisans, and if they were Partisans, it wouldn't matter.

ALAN. And were they?

JACOB. We didn't know for sure- but either way they were about to shoot us. They blindfolded us and took us to this underground room. It was awful- marching us blindfolded- I could hear my Taté breathing so hard.

ALAN. You must have been terrified.

JACOB. Because I could sense how frightened my father was. And then they led him away into the darkness and took off my blindfold. I was alone with this tall man with a scar on his lip.

PARTISAN LEADER They tell me the man called you Jakov. Is that your name?

JAKOV. My name is Jakov, yes. What is yours?

PARTISAN LEADER. Who was that man?

JAKOV. That man is my father- where is he?

PARTISAN LEADER Is that your name, Jakov?

JAKOV. Yes, of course it is. Where is my Taté? Where have you taken him?

PARTISAN LEADER. Listen to me very carefully, little JAKOV.. I will ask you the questions. Do you understand?

JAKOV. Yes, but please, where is my father?

PARTISAN LEADER. Where were you going? Why were you in the woods?

JAKOV. We are going to bring my sister home. Are you German?

PARTISAN LEADER. I said I will ask the questions. Why were you not on the road?

JAKOV. The Germans are along the roads. We are hiding from them like you. Are you Russian? My sister, she writes for the Russian newspaper; she is a reporter. We are walking, and we must hurry-

PARTISAN LEADER. You are walking all the way to Wolozin?

JAKOV. Yes.

PARTISAN LEADER. That is very far. Where are you really going?

JAKOV. We are going to Wolozin.

PARTISAN LEADER. And who is that man we found with you?

JAKOV. That is my Taté. My father. He is a good man. Everyone knows my Taté. He makes shoes and takes photographs-

PARTISAN LEADER. He takes photographs?

JAKOV. When someone in the shtetl dies and at weddings.

PARTISAN LEADER. Where is his camera?

JAKOV. At home. He did not need it today. No one has died.

PARTISAN LEADER. And no one is getting married. Why does he speak German?

JAKOV. My father does not speak German. He speaks Yiddish like me- and Russian. We live in Rubiezewicze.

PARTISAN LEADER. Why does this photographer speak German?

JAKOV. He doesn't. Why do you keep saying things that aren't true!

PARTISAN LEADER. Because we need for you to tell us the truth. Now who is he, and who are you? If this man was really your father he would not take such a young boy into the woods to walk all the way to Wolozin. It is too dangerous. He is a fool!

JAKOV. He is not a fool! He is a good father! He is the best father! He brings us food and kisses us and everyone loves his shoes. He is my Father, and we are going to Wolozin, and you better let us go! Do you hear me? Let us go!

JACOB. And the man walked away, and a few minutes later the two other men brought my father back in to see me. And he was shivering and covered with sweat. I jumped into his arms and started kissing him all over.

TALL PARTISAN. You are lucky. You screamed very loud and very persuasively. You must really like your father.

SHORT PARTISAN. Come with us. You must go.

TALL PARTISAN. You did something very dangerous. You fell asleep.

SHORT PARTISAN. One of you must stay awake at all times. This is very important.

TALL PARTISAN. You must never walk close together. Always keep some distance from each other. My name is Hershel. I'm from Kojdanow. Some day you'll visit me, and you'll meet my little brother. He is about your age. Your father is a good man, and you are a good boy.

JAKOV. I want to be a Partisan! I want to be on a mission like you!

TALL PARTISAN. You take care of your father and sister; that is your mission. *(He salutes Jakov, and Jakov returns the salute.)*

JACOB.
That night we finally made it to Wolozin, and a Christian family that knew my father let us sleep in their barn. When I woke up, Sarah was sitting near me stroking my hair.

JAKOV.
I am glad you are here. Now we won't have to go all over Wolozin and get killed trying to find you.

SARAH.
It is good to see you, too, little brother.

JAKOV.
Stop kissing me so much!!! You'll wake father!

JACOB.
The Christian family had gone after her for us, and we were so grateful, but then we had to leave. If we had been found at their house, even by their own son who was training to be a guard, it would have been very dangerous for them. So after a quick breakfast, we were back in the woods.

DAVID.
Keep walking.

JAKOV.
They took us for German spies.

SARAH. Who are they?

JAKOV. Partisans! Partisans! You're not listening. A tall one, Yankel, a short one, and one with a cut lip. He was nasty. He was the leader. But he didn't scare me. He kept saying I was lying! That Pappa was speaking German in the other room!

SARAH. The other room?

DAVID. They separated us. Interrogated us.

SARAH. How awful. You must have been so frightened.

JAKOV. Not me! I said bring me back my Taté! Right now!

DAVID. I was certain they were going to shoot me.  They kept asking for my camera. I never did know how they knew I took photographs. *(Jakov looks at the ground but says nothing.)* Then they left me alone for a moment, and all I could think was this is it. This is where I am going to die.

JAKOV. Taté, keep walking…

DAVID. Then they came back, and said "You are lucky to have your little boy with you. He was very convincing."

JAKOV. See! I told them: "Let us go!"

DAVID. And to think I almost left to bring you back alone. Without Yankele… I was sure it was wrong to take him, and yet if I hadn't…

JAKOV. I told you. I can run fast and scream loud. I am very useful!

DAVID. We have a decision to make, so let us sit here and tell me what you want to do. Should we separate or stay close together?

JAKOV. Herschel said to stay far apart! Father!

DAVID. I know.

SARAH. Herschel?

JAKOV. The tall one. The Partisan. Someday you will listen to what I have to say. You'd like him Sarah. He was the one who brought father back in. He was sooo big!

DAVID.*(Something is heard in the bushes.)* Ssh, Yakov. Be very quiet, please. Now we must always have a plan. This is what we will do. We must stay close together, close enough not to lose sight of each other but far enough apart that we can run away if the Germans stop one of us. *(The tall Partisan can be seen shadowing them as they begin to move. They do not see him.)* We must run deeper into the forest if that happens. No matter what. If they stop one of us, the others go. Is that clear?

JACOB. No matter what- if they stop one of us, the others go…. My father always had a plan. Every time they moved us, from camp to camp, he would sit with me and plan a strategy… *(He sighs again.)*

ALAN. Here, take some more water.

JACOB. No, no. My teeth. If I drink too much water, my teeth will become too loose. You don't want for my teeth to fall out in your office.

ALAN. Please. Put them on my desk if you have to. So you got home all right with Sarah?

JACOB. Oh yes. And mother and Bobie and the little ones were so happy. This is what is so hard to believe. In the middle of so much that was terrible, we were able to feel so much joy. Laughing and singing and carrying on- Many years ago, but I still hear them singing… and laughing… Forgive me, but I am talking so much again. And you have so much work to do.

ALAN. Jacob, I've been thinking. I want to try and help you, you know that, but- well, I'm just not sure that I can.

JACOB. I understand you are very busy-

ALAN. No, it's not just that. I make time for things I care about- there is always time-

JACOB. For some, I am not getting younger, you know.

ALAN. I know. And I would very much like to help- I know there is nothing more important to you than your sister's work.

JACOB. It is my mitzvah. Do you know this word?

ALAN. Yes, I think. Like in bar mitzvah, right?

JACOB. It means commandment or obligation. It is my mission-

ALAN. See, you are talking to the only Jew who doesn't even know what Mitzvah means… *(Turns to his Jewish friend Deb.)* How pathetic is that?

DEB. You didn't know Mitzvah?

ALAN. No, Deb. And I don't like lox.

28

DEB. That is pathetic.

ALAN. I mean how silly is it that this poor sweet man, this devout Jew, this survivor who has been through so much, so much- and what have I survived- Reagan… is spilling his story to me- To me? I mean, I am almost an anti-Semitic Jew. I don't practice, I barely believe. In fact, I get so angry sometimes at the whole notion of Jewishness, I want to scream.

DEB. Maybe that is the point. Did you tell him this?

ALAN. Yes- *(back to Jacob.)* alright I am going to say this, and I hope you don't get upset. I mean since we don't know each other all that well yet.

JACOB. I understand. Speak, please, freely.

DEB. What did you say?

ALAN. I told him that I'm not sure that I could do justice to the story- his sister's story because *–(to Jacob now)* unlike your sister Sarah, I have a real problem with religious nations. But this goes beyond just separation of synagogue and state. To be blunt, the whole problem with Israel is our Jewishness, our need to be Jews. The whole problem with religion is the need to be one thing and not another, to separate us from them, and it is this separateness, this belonging, this ideological and theological country club mentality that causes all the problems- the hatred, the persecution. I mean they all have it- the great religions. It is their mother's milk. They all have this exclusivity clause built right in. We are the chosen people. Christ is the only road to everlasting peace. How alluring, how narcotic. But it is those very same differences- those perks which make the flock supposedly special, that make others persecute and hate and burn you alive.

DEB. You said this to him? Did his teeth stay in?

ALAN. Yes, and he did the most amazing thing.

DEB. What?

ALAN. He listened. He thought, and then he said-

JACOB. I understand. I understand what you are saying. And this is why you are the right one to tell this story.

ALAN. I mean, how do you argue with someone who won't argue? *(Back to Jacob.)* I am the right person? Jacob, I am telling you I believe the Jews probably do not belong in Israel. I am telling you that it is our very

Jewishness that keeps getting us into trouble. I am telling you that I am not worthy of telling this most holy of holy stories.

JACOB. Let me tell you something. May I tell you something?

ALAN. Yes, please go ahead.

JACOB. God will allow it. God wants you to tell this story-

ALAN. But Jacob, what if I do not believe there is a God?

JACOB. Let me finish. I am speaking? No? Whether you believe there is a God or not, I am here no? You do not ask me to leave, do you? No. Because you are a good man, and you believe that Sarah's story is important.

ALAN. And yours. Your story is important as well.

JACOB. Fine, but my story is Sarah's story. They are one in the same. As is yours. And God knows this, and God sees this, and this is why he has sent me to you.

ALAN. *(To his friend DEB.)* So now I have to argue with God. This play is being written as a mitzvah by a boy who wasn't even Bar Mitzvahed.

DEB. What if he's right? I mean, what if this is what is supposed to happen? Something is attracting you to this story, no? So maybe it is not from a spiritual, divine place, but from an ontological place- you dealing with our own past and inability to reconcile your own sense of self- sort of place.

ALAN. Oh, that makes me feel much better-

JACOB. This was my destiny. I cannot argue with it. I did not choose it. It happens to us, you see. My father, my beloved Taté, he made sure I would stay alive, why? So that I will find the diary. Someone in the family had to survive so that Sarah's diary could be saved.

ALAN. But WHY! Why you, why not Sarah? I mean why did she have to die so that all we have is her diary? Why if there is a God did he have to take Sarah- and so many others for that matter?

JACOB. This is not for us to ask why.

ALAN. No, do not give me that!  I am. I am asking why! And so was she! And that is what I love about your sister, that as devout as she was, as holy as she was, she still had the guts to say WHY! Why Lord?! And if she didn't get an answer then maybe it was because there is no Lord!

JACOB. And that is exactly why she perished.

ALAN. Because there is no God?

JACOB. Because she doubted.

ALAN. What? WHAT? Are you going to sit here and tell me, forgive me, but I can't believe this- are you going to tell me because your sister doubted, she had to die? Are you telling me that not once, not once in all these years you haven't doubted? When they had you in their camps? When they bomb Israel, when they take out the World Trade Center? Not once- not once have you wondered- well maybe this God stuff is all a bunch of hooey?

JACOB. No. Forgive me, but not once. Never. Do you know the story of Moses?

ALAN. Yes. Most of it.

JACOB. Do you know how he died?

ALAN. No, I didn't even know mitzvah remember-

JACOB. On a mountain Nebo in the desert overlooking the Promised Land. He was allowed to see but not allowed to cross over. And do you know why? Because in the middle of the desert, he failed to do God's will. He struck a stone to make water and so as horrible as it sounds, as tragic as it must have been for God-

ALAN. Not to mention Moses.

JACOB. Because he failed to obey- God could not allow Moses into the Promised Land.

ALAN. Oh come on, how parental, how patriarchal! So this great holy man, Moses, leads the entire Jewish people out of slavery. This stuttering farmer rescues an entire population and then leads them through the desert starving and homeless for forty years- and God says "sorry no dice, you pissed me off one day"- one day in forty years- "and so Paradise is not yours. Get up on the mountain and look but don't touch?" What kind of God is that? What ever happened to forgiveness? To devotion? I'm sorry Jacob, but if this is your God, if this is the God that took your beautiful loving and devoted sister, because she was in despair for one day, what good is he? No wonder everyone is killing in the name of such Gods, blind with faith- these are faiths rooted in pain and despair.

DEB. And what did he say to that.

ALAN. He bowed his head for the longest time. He said nothing for what seemed to be forever. Wrestling with the guilt of his sister's death, like Jacob and the angel. I went online Deb- and I looked up the story of Moses because I couldn't believe it could be true and do you know what the name of the place is – where Moses had his crisis of faith?

DEB. No, and I don't like lox either by the way.

ALAN. It was at a place called Kadesh and it became known as Meribah which means strife, disagreement, discord. Meribah Kadesh, the waters of discord. It was an oasis in the middle of the desert, or at least it was after Moses struck the rock and turned it into one. His people were dying of thirst and this had happened before. I mean after all, he had thousands of people wandering through the desert, and already been allowed to draw water from one stone by striking it, but this time when he asked the Lord, the Lord's reply was for him to take up his staff and speak to the stone. Speak to it but don't strike it. But for some reason, and only Moses knows why, maybe because he was a stutterer, he hit the stone with the staff and at first- no water. So he struck it again and finally water flowed. So, lo and behold, he did indeed draw water from the rock, and he saved his people. But God forbid, and I mean that quite literally, and I understand why this is such an overused Jewish phrase now, this time by disobeying the Lord on what would seem a point of technicality - he sealed his fate forever. He would never set foot in the Promised land.  At Meri-bah-kadesh, a little oasis of water in the middle of the desert. Meri-bah-kadesh, the Waters of Discord.

JAKOV. Why are we stopping here. We need to get to the mill and bring back the flour.

SARAH. Because it is beautiful here. The setting sun over the water. See the reflection… Countless jewels on the water…

JAKOV. Stop dreaming, Sarah. Let's go.

SARAH. Nothing in the world is more beautiful than this…

JAKOV. Come on, the sun is- just the sun, doing what the sun is supposed to do-

SARAH. See how calmly the water flows. If you listen very carefully you can hear it. Do you hear? And the birds singing. A symphony is being written just for us.

JAKOV. The water is good for fishing and swimming, yes, but you make a big geschete about everything.

SARAH. Because we are outside and far away, we've escaped from everything terrible. Look, look around.

JAKOV. We are outside because I snuck into the mill and risked my neck and earned some flour for us to eat, but I couldn't carry it all-

SARAH. There is so much beauty, so much artistry in the world… All around are paintings, and music, we have never been to a museum, but I cannot imagine they could be any richer- I am sure of it. I have never been to a concert but listen to this music! I feel like dancing.

JAKOV. You are going to make us late. You are supposed to be helping me carry the flour. Stop dancing with me and let's go.

SARAH. Dance with me, Jakov, please, just this once.

JAKOV. If I dance, will you promise to hurry and go? Taté said it was dangerous if we are caught.

SARAH. I know. I know.

> *They dance. Music again is playing as if written and performed for Sarah to dance to.*

JAKOV. Why did we have to remove our stars? I like my star. And I am good at sneaking inside. I got the flour.

SARAH. Yes, you are very resourceful-

JAKOV. I'm sneaky-

SARAH. Like a little blonde mouse you are, my sneaky little brother of a mouse. Oh, if anyone can survive this you will.

> *They dance some more.*

JAKOV. Sarah, explain what is going on.

SARAH. We're dancing by the river.

JAKOV. No, I mean with the Germans and the Jews.

SARAH. Who can explain? The Germans want to kill all of us.

JAKOV. Kill us? Kill us. But why?

SARAH. Because we are Jews. And we are evil.

> *The music stops.*

JAKOV. I think you need to see a doctor. Something terrible has happened to you.

SARAH. Jakov, why do you think you had to hide in the forest when you went to bring me home?

JAKOV. We are not evil! You should have never come back. If this is what you think.

SARAH. This is not what I think, it is what they think.

JAKOV. You are crazy!

SARAH. Listen, Jakov, you know what I'm saying is true. And I know it makes no sense, and I know it is terrifying-

JAKOV. That is just the sun, and this is just a river, and who dances in the middle of a field? And why would anyone want to kill Taté and Bobie? Why would anyone want to kill us all?

SARAH. Jakov-

> *He runs off.*

SARAH. I wanted to remain standing where I was for a long time and to observe the calm, now quiescent life of nature. I wanted to transform myself into a completely lifeless being entirely unaware of anything, so that everything would be ended for me. All my young days would then have been in the past, all that I was to experience would have been experienced, all the joys of life would have been over and cut off as I was, all questions would have been answered, clearly and understandably; all my secret, never uttered to anyone thoughts would have remained deep in my heart, gone with me forever. Yet one thinks: No! One must go on living. Really to see true happiness some day.

> *Jakov is covered in flour and being helped by a beautiful Christian-Polish girl.*

JAKOV. What are you doing?

KHANE. I'm helping you.

JAKOV. Do you know who I am?

KHANE. You are Jakov. Though it is hard to tell under all that flour. Here.

JAKOV. Stop. You must leave it alone.

KHANE. Don't worry. I'm not going to hurt you.

JAKOV. I must not be seen here.

KHANE. I know that.  You are very brave. I was wondering if you would be back.

JAKOV. I've come for my flour. *(Their eyes meet. Jakov moves her pigtail that has fallen in front of her face.)* Don't worry I'm not going to hurt you….

SARAH. Khane, how nice to see you.

JAKOV. This is my sister, Sarah.

SARAH. Hello.

JAKOV. This is –

SARAH. I know, Khane. Getzel, the miller's daughter. You are a very beautiful young lady, Khane. Don't you think so, Jakov?

KHANE. You look like a boy with all your hair gone.

JAKOV. It is under her hat. She often dresses like a boy. She has turned crazy lately. We don't know what to do with her…

GETZEL. Khane, what are you doing?

KHANE. Helping, Jakov and his sister.

GETZEL. Take the flour you earned, but you must leave, please. Get out of here as fast as you can.

  *He takes Khane away.*
SARAH. She is a beautiful girl.

JAKOV. She makes my head ache.

SARAH. She likes you. I can tell by the way she was looking at you.

JAKOV. When she was helping me with the flour our eyes met, and I wanted to say something to her, but I got all choked up. It was so odd. Then my heart started to pound, and in my pants, I cannot tell you what else happened but ---Why? We weren't fighting, and I don't even like girls.

SARAH. Not even Fanya?

JAKOV. Especially not Fanya. She is the one who follows me around. Why are you smiling at me? You think I am funny? I should never have told you. I don't know why I talk to you at all.

SARAH. I know you are being serious. I just forget how old you are getting. You will be a young man soon. Soon you will celebrate your Bar-Mitzvah. We will all be so proud of you.

> *Jacob knocks on the door to Alan's office as he did at the beginning of the play.*

JACOB. Alan. We have so much work to do-

ALAN. Jacob, we were meeting this Friday, were we not?

JACOB. Yes, but by Friday we could be finished, no?

ALAN. This is so odd I was just going to call you to reschedule. See, things-

JACOB. No need I am here. Alan, my granddaughter, she must play Sarah. Now I know I have a prejudice here, but she read the Torah, my God you should have seen her. Sarah would have been so proud… She even looked like Sarah… Now I know it is not my place, but if you ever finish, when you put on this play, we should think of having her play Sarah.

ALAN. We'll see.

JACOB. What is wrong? This is only a suggestion. I know that the decision will be other people's. And I have also been thinking maybe this needs to be more than one play- we have so much-

ALAN. Jacob, maybe we should get through with Act One in the first play before we plan the mini-series.

JACOB. I'm sorry. I will come back on Friday.

ALAN. No, it is my wife. I haven't been able to work on the play because we have had to go to doctor after doctor. She isn't feeling well, so-

JACOB. I am so sorry, what is it?

ALAN. They don't know yet. She has shortness of breath, and she coughs all the time. They think it might be a virus or pneumonia.

> *Alan's wife, a non Jew from another country, appears and is talking with him.*

KATE. They think it might be a virus or pneumonia. I have to go back next Friday for a CAT scan. Will you go with me?

ALAN. Sure, of course. Damn.

KATE. What?

ALAN. Nothing. I just have an appointment I'd have to change. With Jacob. I'll just tell him I'm too busy. I've been looking for a reason to get out of this; I just don't know how to tell him...

JACOB. I will ask all I know to say special prayers for her.

KATE. Be nice to him. It's not his fault you don't know how to say no.

ALAN. *(to Jacob)* Thank you. So why did you come here today? Not that I'm not glad to see you. Oh, and please let me apologize for last week.

JACOB. Not at all. No need. It is I that should apologize to you... *(He begins to tear up.)*

ALAN. Would you like some water?

JACOB. No, my teeth...you should have seen my granddaughter...so beautiful...but her mother, my daughter...I'm not sure I should be talking so- it is perhaps not appropriate-

ALAN. Please, whatever you need to say.

JACOB. I feel like I can speak about such things with you-

ALAN. Good, I'm glad. I will send you my bill next month.

JACOB. Yes…anyway my daughter. She and I have not been close for some time. Since my wife and I no longer are married.

ALAN. How long ago was that?

JACOB. Oh, years now-fifteen, twenty. Anyway, she loves me- this is not the problem, but she doesn't- well, I am not easy to be around, as you know. She doesn't like to spend very much time with me, and my granddaughter- she barely knows me. I guess, you see, she feels that I am living too much in the past. "Pappa," she says, "please not again. We know these horrible things, but not today please!"

ALAN. Why, what happened?

JACOB. I showed her the script. The pages you had written. I wanted her to know how happy I was that someone was going to tell Sarah's story, and she just shook her head. "This is not about you today, Pappa. This is about your granddaughter, and it is a joyful time. This is a new century, and you need to leave that century behind. Leave all those terrible times behind…" And maybe she is right…How silly I was to interrupt such a joyful celebration…

ALAN. Silly? That is exactly what the celebration is for.

JACOB. You think?

ALAN. To remember, to pay homage and pass on tradition. You were not silly.

JACOB. When I arrived at the shul, I saw this woman wearing this great big hat. You know like some movie star pulled way down over one eye-- huge brim. And she hardly looked at me but was walking all around the congregation, and as she sat down, this woman in this tremendous hat- I thought "who would wear such a thing to shul?" Then she sat in the front row, next to me, and I realized it was my daughter. I hardly recognized her…So after the ceremony, I went to the receiving line and was making my congratulations, and I gave my daughter the pages, and I told her about our work. And she said that it was very nice, and we could talk about it later. So at the reception, I saw her walking around- that hat dipping this way and that, and I followed it and found a chair in the corner to talk, but she stood. And said how nice it was for me to come all this way that it meant so much to Hannah. And then she asked if I was getting more sleep.

ALAN. You have trouble sleeping?

JACOB. All my life… I sleep better now, sometimes five or six hours even. But most nights are… they seem so long…

SUNNY. So are you sleeping any better, Pappa?

ALAN. Forgive me, but we have to stop here.

SUNNY. Stop?

ALAN. Yes, we are going to have to cut this scene.

SUNNY and the ENSEMBLE. Cut it? Whoa…Ohh…Why?

ALAN. Hey, part of the problem of working on a play with folks that are real is that- well go ahead, read this letter and you'll see…

SUNNY. Dear Alan. Thanks for sending me a copy of Jude.

ALAN. No, I don't mean read it aloud- oh hell- go ahead that might be the easiest way.

SUNNY. I am very supportive of holocaust education efforts not the least because I spend significant amounts of volunteer time working on them myself. So I certainly wish you the best of luck in achieving your goal to develop and use holocaust related quote creative events unquote as a means to quote foster dialogue rather than intolerance unquote. The success of a project such as yours will rest, in large part, on the authenticity and the credibility of the materials you use in carrying it out. It will, of course, also rest on the integrity of the people who are its representatives and spokespersons, For all these reasons, I feel compelled to write to you about my reaction to "Jude." Jude contains a brief reference to my daughter's Bat Mitzvah and to my immediate family's personal history, and while doing so, purports to relate specific conversations, occurrences and facts. While I appreciate that from your dramatist's point of view, those purported conversations, occurrences and facts help to make Jacob a highly sympathetic protagonist, they are actually figments of the imagination. *(The actress pauses)* Well duh…*(Resumes reading)* For the record: My daughter did have a Bat Mitzvah, my father did see and hear her read from the Torah, I did wear a black hat, my parents are divorced, my father quote is not an easy man to live with unquote, I don't quote like to spend very much time with unquote my father, my daughter quote barely knows unquote my father, and, in my youth, I did have the nickname Sunny among my friends.

However, and simply in the order in which the following items appear in the play:

My daughter resembles my husband's side of the family, not mine, so she does not in fact look anything like Sarah.

My father and I have quote not been close unquote since long before my parents ever divorced.

I have never felt, or expressed to anyone an opinion that my father is or ever was quote living too much in the past unquote.

I have never in my life, in any situation, called or referred to my father as Poppa.

I have no history of discussions, let alone repeated discussions, with my father about quote these horrible things unquote and, in fact, didn't actually even learn the most basic facts of his concentration camp and liberation experience until I sat in on an interview he gave when I was in college.

The black hat that I wore on the morning of my daughter's Bat Mitzvah was hardly quote great big, tremendous, huge or worn like some movie star pulled way down over one eye unquote. It was, in fact, a normal sized hat of the sort that is not uncommonly worn in the synagogue.

My father never sat in the front row during either the Friday night or Saturday morning services and we did not at any time sit next to one another or even in the same row with one another. He arrived quite late for both services and on both occasions sat himself apart from the rest of the family.

I have never asked him about his sleeping habits at any time before during or after the Bat Mitvah, and indeed, have never at any time in my life had any conversation with him about his sleeping habits, past or present.

My father has never, at any time in my life, called me Sunny and I have never, at any time in my life, referred to myself by that name when talking to him.

I have never said to my father or to anyone else quote it would be good of you to come unquote or quote so nice of you to come unquote because that isn't the sort of syntax I use.

*(The actress breaks away from the letter)* Clearly…

*(And resumes)* My father was several years older than 24, not 24, and my mother was 23, not 20, when they married.

My mother divorced my father for reasons way more serious than the statement quote I am not an easy person to live with unquote suggests.

Alan, I do not have any personal knowledge of any pre-war or war related experiences of my father or any member of his immediate family. Obviously I wasn't there. I also do not have any personal knowledge of what is said in Sarah's diary. I have never seen the document and in any event, I don't read Yiddish, so it is impossible for me to personally verify the faithfulness of the translation.

However I was at my daughter's Bat Mitvah, and so I have personal, direct knowledge about everything that I saw and did there. Based on that knowledge, I can tell you equivocally that none of the experiences portrayed as having taken place during that times and as involving me actually took place. None.

What that tells me, and what I think it should tell you, is that to the extent you are relying on my father as your quote historical consultant unquote and/or the sole source of your material, beware. You should take care to fact check, particularly when the material, including Jude, refers to living people by their real names, and is presented in a context that would reasonably lead the reader/listener/viewer to conclude that it is a faithful retelling of an accounting of events that actually transpired.

With best wishes for a happy and healthy new year, Sincerely Son-

ALAN. No, no…

SUNNY. *(makes up a name)* Betty… Fishkin.

JACOB. She's a very good lawyer.

ALAN. Jacob, I am so sorry.

JACOB. *(Trying to shrug it off)* Ahhh…this is the way things have turned out, what can you do about them. Both of my children... And my wife. Ex-wife…Let's be honest, we were too young when we got married. Like so may others of our day. We lived together for many years; we did share a life together; I raised a family. Two successful children-

STUDENT. *(to another student)* Who apparently won't speak to him…

JACOB. But as I said, I am not an easy person to live with… I guess to have a husband that sleeps soundly is not too much to ask for…

KATE. Are you going to be home at all this weekend? Bill and Stan are coming over. Do you want me to make us dinner?

ALAN. Sure. Jacob is away. So I gave the cast the weekend off.

KATE. So kind of Jacob to go away …

ALAN. Oh, come on Kate. I told him I'd have more pages ready when he got back. See why do I keep telling him that?

KATE. Don't ask me, Alan. You know what I think.

ALAN. That it's just theater, who cares.

KATE. I'm going to ignore that. Because you're tired…

ALAN. I just asked for a little advice.

KATE. You always ask, or pretend to ask- should I or shouldn't I, and then you do it anyway. Face it, when it comes to theater when was the last time you actually said no? So stop agonizing over it.  I will edit the pages. I will correct the commas and the many misspelled words like I always do-

ALAN. But it is still just a play-

KATE. No, Alan, it's life. It's someone's real life this time. So don't ask me to be there…

ALAN. What is wrong with you?

KATE. Don't ask me to be there to watch it.

ALAN. I'm not just writing this for Jacob, I am writing this for you.

KATE. I don't want it. I know exactly how his daughter feels.

ALAN. But it's a gift-

KATE. No it's not. It's not a gift; it is a violation.

JACOB. So I came here to tell you that if you did not want to finish the play that I would be very unhappy, but that I would certainly understand. I ask too much of too many people, and this is something that I have learned…

ALAN. *(Remembering.)* You cannot transcend what you do not acknowledge.

JACOB. I'm sorry?

DEB. *(Alan and her alone)* You cannot transcend what you do not acknowledge.

ALAN. Well, that explains it…

DEB. You say that you don't want to write this story, and yet you argue with your beautiful wife about it. You say you want no part in perpetuating the myth of Judaism, and yet you keep meeting with your students and working on this story- vhy iz zis? Because it is a part of you, like it or not. And part of moving on as a person, part of healing, part of the evolution of all cultures, of civilization itself, is acknowledging. Paying respect. Understanding from whence we come. And I say to you brother Alan, that you and I will never transcend anything that we cannot acknowledge. Praise the Lord and pass the peanuts!

ALAN. *(Back to Jacob)* Jacob, go away! Go on. Go. Please. I've got a lot of work to do if I have to finish the first act by Friday.

JACOB. Only the first act?

> *A loud scream is heard from far away. And then more, and then many more. We are back in the Fishkin home.*

SARAH. What is going on?

MERE-LIEBE and YITZHOK. Mamma, Mamma

SHOSHKA. Hush little ones. Sarah, take your brother and sister.

BOBIE. It is the police. They are taking more of the men. Off to work they say. They leave to work, and they never come back. The other day it was in Koydanov. Hundreds were led away. There are rumors they were all shot.

SARAH. Where is Pappa-

JAKOV. He is still in the forest, at Wojeck's house. I'll go.

> *A loud knock is heard. No one moves. Again a knock. Shoshke goes to answer the door.*

POLICEMAN. David Fishkin, please. Where is David Fishkin?

SHOSHKE. He is not here. I'm terribly sorry.

POLICEMAN. Not here? Were is he?

SHOSHKE. I was ill. He went to the next village to get some medicine.

POLICEMAN. No one is to leave. You are under orders.

JAKOV. She was very sick.

SHOSHKE. Jakov! We are sorry.

POLICEMAN. That is his name?

SHOSHKE. Who?

POLICEMAN. The boy.

SHOSHKE. Yes, my son. Jakov.

POLICEMAN. Have him report outside immediately.

SHOSHKE. No!

POLICEMAN. Immediately!

SARAH. He is just a boy.

SHOSHKE. Take me instead. I will go.

POLICEMAN. I suppose you want the Germans to come and burn the whole village to the ground. We are ordered to have one from each house. One man.

SHOSHKE. But sir, please. I can do so much more work.

POLICEMAN. You are sick. The boy will come.  I do not wish to do this. But do as I say, or this whole house will perish. Do not make the Germans any angrier. It will be terrible for us all. Now, prepare some warm clothes for the boy and some food. If he is not there when his name is called he will be shot by the Germans. I will wait outside. You have only a few minutes. Otherwise he goes right now, the way he is.

BOBIE. We will do as you say Officer, thank you for your understanding.

> *The policeman leaves and we hear names being called out. Name after name. They continue throughout the next few lines. As a name is called someone joins the line. Sarah is buttoning Jakov's coat.*

SARAH. Don't you worry, my little yellow mouse. Nothing will happen to you.

*Chaim Lotus!*

SARAH. This will pass, you will see. The Germans will be destroyed and nothing will happen to you.

*Berl Chavitz!*

SARAH. Your instinct for self preservation will tell you when to run and how to survive.

JAKOV. Instinct. What is instinct? Is it a person? What does he look like?

*Yankef Motes!.*

JAKOV. Is he a Partisan? A ghost? The Messiah? How will I know him?

*Laibe Yankels.*

SARAH.  You remember how your Betar leader caught a rabbit?

JAKOV. Yes, with a bow and arrow, and we enjoyed eating it.

*Ruve Itzaks.*

SARAH. But the rabbit didn't just sit there and wait to be caught, he ran didn't he?

JAKOV. Yes, very fast.

SARAH. He ran because he sensed danger. That is instinct.

*Mote Tamares!  Shoshke and Bobie arrive with a bundle of food and clothes.*

JAKOV. He tried to run in a zig-zag… but he was trapped.

SHOSHKE. Oh my little Yankele, my child, I don't know what to do.

JAKOV. Don't cry, Mamma. I'm going to be all right. I will run faster than any rabbit.

*Boruch Shimons.*

JAKOV. Zig and zag deep into the woods, and I'll find my way back home. I'm a big boy now.  They think of me as an adult. That is why I'm here.

*Ruveh Gottels! She is clinging to him sobbing.*

JAKOV. Mamala, let me go. I don't mind leaving. I will make my own decisions from here on out.

> *The names have stopped. Jakov joins the end of the line. After a beat of silence, Bobie grabs Jakov out of the line.*

BOBIE. They did not call his name. They did not call it. Go Jakov, hurry. Leave and go back to the house. Hurry!!

> *Jakov ducks through the women and hurries off and they stay and pretend to say goodbye to some of the men.*

MAGDA. Jacob Fishkin?

JACOB. Yes. Yes, I am here.

> *The lobby of the International Yiddish Archive, where Alan has been waiting for almost a half an hour.*

ALAN. Oh, thank God. You weren't here; I was worried.

JACOB. The trains were all stopped... I was trapped on the subway.

ALAN. *(Whispering)* It's okay. They've kept me waiting for awhile anyway. Did you bring-

JACOB. Of course. *(To the woman who called his name.)* Forgive me.

ALAN. Yes-

MAGDA. Yes, well good afternoon.  I am Magda. Magda Vittstein, assistant archivist here at the archive.

ALAN. But our appointment was with the director. Mr. Rheins.

MAGDA. Yes, he was called away. He has asked me to meet with you. *(Haughty)* And you are?

JACOB. This is Alan, Alan-

ALAN. Klutzenburg.

MAGDA. Klutzenburg?

ALAN. I am working with Mr. Fishkin, writing a theatrical version of Sarah's diary.

MAGDA. Oh, like the Diary of Anna Frank.

ALAN. Well, yes, but different.

JACOB. You must see it, Miss Vittstein. This will be a very important play.

MAGDA. I'm sure. But we do not produce plays. We have no budget for such things.

ALAN. No, no. We are working on a play, but that is not why we are here.  I thought it was important to find a home for the diary and for Jacob's memoirs.

JACOB. *(We are now a few weeks earlier)* I have done this Alan. I have tried all of the Jewish organizations and archives many times years ago.

ALAN. But I called this International Yiddish archive and they agreed to meet with us.

JACOB. They will not care. You will see-

ALAN. We will make them care. Jacob the diary needs a home. You will not live forever, even if you are doing a very good job of trying.  After you, and I, are long gone the diary must be read.

SARAH. What are we going to do with the diary? What will become of it?

*Back in the Fishkin home.*

JAKOV. I will take it with me. When I fight with the Partisans. I will hide it deep in the woods.

DAVID. We could give it to one of the Gentile families. The farmers, they will hide it.

SHOSHKE. Or the good priest at the Church that helped the refugees from Koydanov.

SARAH. It will be lost. I just know it. All my work. Why must this happen to us.

DAVID. Sarah, don't worry....

SARAH. No one will know how we suffered. And lived. How we laughed and cried.

ALAN. Where is it now?

*Back to Alan and Jacob alone.*

JACOB. I keep it in a safe deposit box. I visit it often and sit with it.

ALAN. Who will visit with it after you are gone? It does not belong in a vault. This archive may publish it. In Yiddish- and English. You have had it translated-

JACOB. Yes, hardly anyone could read it.

ALAN. And if it is published thousands, millions can read it. Is this not what Sarah wanted?

JACOB. Of course. This is what God wanted. This is why I survived.

ALAN. Then let's meet with this director. This is the largest Yiddish archive in the world. Scholars come from all over.

MAGDA. *(Back in the Archive)* Of course we have thousands of holocaust materials. Letters, documents, even some diaries. And quite a number of collections of material. A collection is when we have a substantial group of documents from a given city or area or an important donation from one particular donor deemed significant. Here is the first volume of the catalogue of Eastern European mid-twentieth century material. And we can look up under Poland- 1930s, and you will see how much there is here. And these are the shelves where we keep the material. Each collection has its own section and box-

ALAN. Look at it all.

MAGDA Yes. We have a very thorough representation. The Institute is the premier collection of Yiddish documents in the world. Even more than the center in Jerusalem.

ALAN. You should have seen it, Deb. Box after box, shelf after shelf, like a mausoleum of words....It was so cold and ordered; the air was caustic. And she brought us into the reading room, and there were a few old Hassidic men mumbling toward the pages of yellowed manuscripts, and nowhere could you feel the families…

BOBIE. The diary stays with me! You are all scattering with the winds. Fine. Jakov wishes to run off to the wood and become a Partisan. David to the farmers to work and hide. You Shoshke a seamstress for the gentiles. Yentel is already gone.

*Back in the Fishkin house.*

DAVID. That is the plan! If we stay together we will perish. They will come for us soon.

BOBIE. If this is what we must do to survive, fine. But the diary will stay with me. I will protect it with my life. What will they want with an old toothless women? Go, go away if you must, but you will visit your Bobie every Friday, this is the least you can do, no?  But the diary will stay with me. At home. It belongs in the home of Gershon!

*Back to the archive.*


ALAN. And then he took it out, Deb, and it was like Raiders of the Lost Ark, I'm telling you. Even if you wanted to, you couldn't help but feel the presence of Yahweh, of something deeply sacred. I couldn't even breathe-

JACOB. Here, please read it.

MAGDA. This is the diary? Thank you. If you will allow me.

ALAN. And she put on these very thick glasses and she began to peruse the pages. Like a jeweler hunting for flaws.  And I looked down at them. The pages and the words seemed like cuneiform and were clearly marked by hand, but the hand was so sure and dignified-

MAGDA. She has beautiful penmanship.

JACOB. Yes.

ALAN. And I thought of my early handwriting teachers and how they struggled with me to get a perfect cursive "c" and what a lost art penmanship now is, and how indelicately she seemed to turn the pages, like reading a paperback novel on the subway. And I realized it was because something Sarah had written had caught her eye. She was not studying it anymore but had become a reader, caught up in the story…

MAGDA. What a beautiful phrase. Her Yiddish is lovely. Very musical. This is obviously a very special document.

ALAN. And then I looked at the cracked, chestnut cover and the binding tearing away, bandages tattered from too much healing, and I noticed how very small it was. Of course it would be small, who would have a large diary? It would not be inviting to carry around a hefty tome. And yet when you think of all that Sarah must have wanted to record, how much was being packed into those eighteen young years. It seemed so slight- like the size of the Mona Lisa after you finally wait in line for hours to see it. A masterpiece in miniature. But then she handed the book back to me instead of Jacob, I have no idea why-

MAGDA. Yes, we would be very honored to have such a document-

ALAN. And I held it for the first time, Sarah's diary, and it was… as if time slipped away. I was sitting in that shtetl with that family about to be torn apart and moments away from destruction. I could see Bobie's toothless grin, and Merrie-Liebbe and Yitzhak, and the book became huge. I could feel the weight of each page, of the ink, of each word, and there were thousands, and all at once it was too much, too heavy to hold. And I dropped it onto the reading desk-

MAGDA. *(Impatiently)* Careful! *(More politely)* Careful there.

ALAN. I'm so sorry.

JACOB. It is all right.

ALAN. And Jacob snatched it up quick as a shortstop as it touched the turf. And I knew then and there he wanted no part of this place.

MAGDA. Perhaps we could include some of your other pieces of writing and name it as a collection after your sister.

JACOB. I appreciate your interest, and I will, of course, think this over.

MAGDA. We understand these are very difficult decisions, but please, be assured we take very good care of our documents. We would microfiche your sister's work, and then it will be protected for up to a hundred years or more. Even when the volume is too fragile to be touched, it can be read on microfiche.

ALAN. Why not scan it and have a digital copy?

MAGDA. Archives do not believe in digital because the software will most assuredly become out of date. The program you are writing your little play on in five years will be obsolete.

ALAN. I see. Well, don't tell Microsoft that.

MAGDA. We archivists preserve; that is our business. Our battle is with time. Each year counts. So the difference between five or ten and a hundred, well, that is quite a victory is it not?

DOCTOR. *(Who appears in a spot of light)* She has lung cancer. Non-small cell carcinoma. There is very little doubt about that. The most important thing is to make sure of the stage. We measure these things in stages and each stage is very significant. It could add years onto the survival rate.

ALAN. I left the Archive and said goodbye to Jacob to get back to work and missed the doctor's phone call by five minutes. One of those "Oh my God, this is just like in the movies" phone calls where he said he thought it would be prudent to come down to his office. He had something he wanted to discuss with Kate and me. I mean of course it was cancer.

DEB. I know all about it. You get a call like that and all of a sudden getting to the doctors, getting across town, is more difficult than a refugee crossing the border.

ALAN. I mean what's up with that? Here I am holding this sacred work. This biblical Old Testament-like book and the very next moment my wife is struck with this life or death sentence. I couldn't help but laugh and then cry at the coincidence. Okay, so maybe there is a God. And Jesus, is He ever vengeful!

> *Loud knocking from all sides of the theater and German being yelled. In German we hear: "Raus, mach schnell, raus, farfluchte Juden." "Out, make it fast, out you damn Jews." "Everyone out, out into the streets immediately." We are transporting you to a work camp. This yelling continues over and over, and a sad old man enters the Fishkin home.*

DAVID. Mr. Eisenbaud? Mr. Eisenbaud. How good to see you.

MR. EISENBAUD. No, please. Do as they say. Prepare yourself to leave. And I have been ordered to take all of the gold that you have in your possession. Please give me all of your gold.

JACOB. They were taking everything. Wedding bands, bracelets, gold watches, necklaces- any and every piece of gold jewelry. Now I knew this man, this Mr. Eisenbaud- he was the head of the Judenrat- the Jewish Council, the go-betweens between the Jews and the Germans. He was an important man. I had ridden on his shoulders. I'd gotten pickled herring and a drop of schnapps from him at parties. And now he was pale and he'd been beaten.

MR. EISENBAUD. We must do this. If we don't they will shoot us for not cooperating.

JACOB. And my father took off his wedding band-

DAVID. Twenty years ago I was the happiest man on earth because you put this ring on my finger; now twenty years later my love for you is just as strong.

JACOB. And gave it to him, and my mother took off her wedding band and gave it to him. Then she tried to remove her earrings and couldn't.

MR. EISENBAUD. Here, let me help you.

JACOB. And he helped her take off her earrings like a lover might. And my mother and father, they embraced Mr. Eisenbaud, the father of our shtetl. And my younger sister and brother ran over to him and kicked him and bit him.

MERRE-LIEBE. Don't you take my mother away!

YITZKHOK. Don't you take my father!

JACOB. And then he turned to Bobie. Now Bobie had so little in the world. Not even teeth. But she did have a gold watch on a gold chain, and even though it no longer worked, she cherished it like it was made of diamonds. She'd let me polish it once a year, and each time she'd warn me not to break the delicate chain. She'd wear it every Shabbes to shul, and inside it had a picture of her husband, my Zeyde, and her when they were young and in that picture was the same gold watch on a chain. And now, this Mr. Eisenbaud was trying to take it from her.

BOBIE. No! No! It's all I have. It's all I own.

MR. EISENBAUD. I give you my solemn word, if I am able, I will personally return this watch to you. I will tell them it does not even work- you will have no need for this.

JACOB. And my father took the watch and gave it to Mr. Eisenbaud.

MR. EISENBAUD. God be with us all.

JACOB. And he was gone. And then my father gave her the picture from inside. He had at least saved that.

DAVID. Here, Bobie, put this in Sarah's diary. And now we, too, must go. It is time.

> *The shouting grows louder now and a music is heard between the shouts. The family gathers together and walks into a long line of people.*

ALAN. And as I was sitting in another waiting room for the second of the second opinions about my wife, it suddenly became so very clear to me. You see, I was reading Jacob's memoirs and at this moment he suddenly switched.  He was no longer writing in prose. And I understood why. He had switched to verse, for in times like this, prose could not hold the events. They would break free of prose, for these emotions only poetry could possibly do…

> *The music comes to the foreground now and the shouts recede and the movement of the actors becomes very symbolic. Whatever is recited by Jacob is seen onstage, the action is, from here until the end of the act, a dance or movement piece, perhaps sung.*

JACOB.
The air is close
The noise is loud,
The Germans use their guns
To keep everyone from leaving

Mother and father come running to us,
Reassuring us many times.


DAVID, SHOSHKE, and JACOB.
You needn't be afraid little ones.
Nothing bad will happen to you—
Not that you have done anything evil;
Everyone knows that,
Soon we shall leave this place
And go home together.

JACOB.
My youngest brother
Handsome and bright,
With your eyes of blue
And your beautiful blond locks.
Your trousers patched,
Your tiny shoes shabby
With their laces knotted.

I hold your delicate little hand,
Your words are indistinct and half spoken,
Your baby voice sounds frightened
And choked with tears.

I lift you up in my outstretched arms,
And feel your little heart
Beating ever so loudly.
I press you to my heart,
Kiss you, and caress you, and I smile.
Fear not, my little brother,
I'll carry you in my arms
And I'll not abandon you.

A sweet smile covers his face
But soon his worn tears repose on my
Cheek,
His trembling little arms are tight around
My throat.
His sharp baby teeth
Bite into my flesh and blood begins
To flow;
His little feet kick
As the Germans tear him from my arms

My young sister, Merre-Liebe—
A nine year old with black eyes
Like cherries
With long unruly curly hair
Which falls across her fine-featured face.
Called the prettiest in her class
And excelling in every subject—
Even now I see you clearly,
Running to Father and Mother
And shouting out to me:

MERRE LIEBE.
"I will not stay here
With all these children!
Take me with you brother!"

JACOB.
Then running back to Mother,
Then to Father, and from SARAH. to me.
I fell to my knees and clasped you tight:

JAKOV
"Do not weep, pretty little sister.
We'll hide you among us.

JACOB.
And the first German did not notice her.
But the sadistic second one
Whipped us with his stick,
Tearing our chain apart.

My poor sister, you fell at our feet.
The German dragged you by your lovely curls,
Pushed and slammed you
In among the other children.
I loved you more than myself,
And oh, how I miss you!
Even now I see you slipping,
From Father to Mother, from SARAH. to me.
Seven hundred- 700 young children
Pudgy and thin, dark hared and blond
With pretty little faces
Clasped each other, hand in little hand.
Tiny infants, unable to walk, or even stand,
Smiling and laughing with so much charm,
Each little one's tongue
Seeking mother's warm breast—
Dotted the cold ground.

You searched for us with your big eyes,
Black, blue and tearful.
You turned your heads to the right and to the
Left:
Where is my brother, the strong one?
My sister, the pretty one?
Where are Mother and Father, Grandma and Grandpa?"

I see you even now—
Seven hundred children pure of heart—
From Nalibakh, Derowna, from Slobodka and Valma,
From Rubzewitz, Iveniets, from Khatova and Grani.

Father then spied his two young ones
And tried to run toward them.
The German blocked his way.
And aimed a gun a him.

Go back, or I'll shoot,

GERMAN GUARD. "Du Jude verfluchte!"

JACOB.
You damned Jew, he shouted.

Sarah my sister, pulled Father back
While I seized Mother's arm.
We looked around, her eyes searching,
For she could not grasp what had just happened.

Torn, dispirited, separated and strewn.
With no packs, no sacks, no will to live,
We once again were driven out onto the teeming
Road.

> *The lights fade on the Fishkins huddled together, Sarah and David supporting Shoshke who has collapsed, Jakov trying to help. They are moving slowly forward.*

**End of Act One**

# ACT TWO

*The Fishkin family is seen moving slowly in the same line as
before. David and Sarah holding up Shoshke, and Jakov nearby.
Jacob in a separate light speaks still using verse, still with a musical
underscore:*

JACOB.
Father on one side, Sarah on the other,
Led her
Through the wood and field, city and village,
Despite storms and frigid snow

DAVID.
We'll bring our little ones back home.
Dear heart be strong!
You are the very beat in my breast,
The air in my lungs
The sun that shines
And warms my soul.

SOLDIER. Macht schnell, macht schnell, ihr verfluchten
Juden!

JACOB.
Hurry up, hurry up you damned Jews!
Came the Germans' strident command once more.
The dust rose again and obscured the sun.

RABBI.
God in Heaven, You give us much sand!
But where is even a bit of rain to settle the dust
And quench our thirst?

JACOB.
So pleaded our neighbor, eyes raised toward the
Sky.

SARAH. Where are you from, Sir?

RABBI. I am a rabbi in the town of Derewna
Neighbor to your shtetl Rubzewitz
And this is my wife, saintly woman.

Permit me, Reb Dovid, to help you
While you rest your weary body.

JACOB.
Lovingly they each took Mother by an arm
And led her, like a bride at a wedding.
With brave words, pious and heartfelt
They strove to imbue her with hope.

She responded with tears and smiles
And thanked them effusively.
Although it hardly seemed possible, they succeeded
In regenerating her soul.

Sarah reached into her rucksack,
For food
And turned to the two caring people

SARAH.
We'll share whatever we have with you.

JACOB.
 The Rabbi's wife spoke:

RABBI'S WIFE.
We cannot accept your food
You have so little for yourselves.
We still have something in our pockets that we can
Eat.

JACOB.
Sarah said:

SARAH.
We have so little, and you have nothing.
We therefore have much more than you do.
To give when one has is indeed a very great mitvah.
But to give when one has nothing—
What is the dimension of such a sacrifice?

RABBI.
What you have given us is much more than food:
Life and courage are your gifts.
And when courage is gone, all is lost.
Does anyone know what will become of us now?

SOLDIER.
Aufstehen! Aufstehen! Schmutzigen Juden!

Get up, get up, you dirty Jews!

JACOB.
Their bark resembled those of wild dogs.
But our way was blocked:
A herd of deer, small and large,
Brown in color, antler spread.
Jammed the winding road.
The Germans, reluctant to chase them,
Uncertain what to do
Began to watch the deer
And forgot about us for a moment
Confused the deer stood still.

Help from God in the guise of deer!
People around us were saying
But their hope was short lived
For the Germans began shooting at the animals.
Swift and graceful, the deer began
To run from us in fear.

RABBI
My dear people: Two Thousand years ago
The Amalekites set out to destroy our ancestors
They ravaged and devastated our land,
Set fire to the Holy Temple
And dispersed our people.

For two thousand years we have been wandering
Over all lands
We have survived pogroms, inquisitions.
We fled
Overseas and over continents,
Seeking a haven and respite

But, dear people, it was all to no avail:
Our reward was anti-Semitism.
Yet the sparks of our Jewish faith remained in our
Hearts.
Remember—never forget—
Who we are,
We are Jews forever.

In our Holy Torah it is written:
Remember Amalek! Never forget!
Multitudes of Amalekites

Disappeared from the earth;
No trace of them remains.
Dear friends, what is the lesson
Of "Remember Amalek"?
It is that our people
Are eternal, a beacon to other nations.
Yes, our Heavenly Father may punish His people
But He will never forsake them.

We must maintain our faith in God.
You shall see: This is but a test.
Recall the story of sacrifice of Isaac.
You shall see: The Lord will protect us.
He will send angels
To crush our foes.

Their names will be erased
From the memory of the world
And we Jews, God's children,
Shall settle in our homeland.
We will build it –plant new trees
Cleanse the Holy Land of ugliness
And bring back milk and honey.
Rise from the ground,
My dear friends,
Hold yourselves erect,
Lift high your heads,

And let us together sing,
Sing our anthem in a unified voice.

*The Rabbi and Sarah begin to sing the Hatikva and one by one the
others join. After one verse, a German fires a gun into the air and
everyone stops singing.*

JACOB.
The fat pasty-faced German,
Strode up to the Rabbi of Derewna.

SOLDIER.
Sag deinen Juden dass wir marchieren müssen.

JACOB.
Tell your Jews we must march!
He commanded.
60

The Rabbi of Derewna, his voice proud
Responded to the pale faced one:

RABBI
Ich habe meinen Juden gesagt was ich schon sagen müsste.

JACOB.
I have already told my Jews what I needed to tell them.

DEB. Where are we going?

> *A traffic median on the Upper West Side.*

ALAN. Kate is meeting us. She wants us to be there.

DEB. Meet us where? How is she doing?

ALAN. Fine. She had three treatments, and she's lost a lot of hair, but she's a fighter.

DEB. She sure is. After three chemos, I was like tapioca pudding.

ALAN. At seven o'clock all over town people are just getting together to pay their respects.

DEB. I heard about this. We used to do that in the sixties, but everyone ended up in bed together so-

> *They have reached a small group of neighbors- the same actors that have played all the other groups of people and everyone has a different kind of candle. Some are giving out candles to others. Someone gives Deb a candle.*

DEB. Thanks. You should see me at dinner parties, I always forget wine.

ALAN. Hey, Sweetheart. How do you feel?

KATE. Fine. A little sore. I'm fine.

DEB. She's a super hero, your wife is.

> *They realize no one else is talking and everyone is just standing quietly. Some are hugging and holding each other. Then some*

*people begin to sing softly. More and more people join in and the group becomes quite large and very peaceful.*

ENSEMBLE. Friday, 3rd April 1942 The Second Day of Passover

SARAH. What does any word signify in our evil time? A word is exactly like a fruit. One must be able to eat it to know the taste of it. "By the individual, the collective will be judged." The collective is alive, the entire large entity is alive, but we do not see it, for we are but the merest thread in the large fabric and are so submerged in the emptiness and the loneliness, in the minutiae and the pettiness of our own selves that we cannot feel the great life of the community. It is as though we were tiny worms that have bored very deeply into the dark chambers and corridors of our own singleness and have no time to break out into the bright world and see the great sun and lovely light.

ALAN. Jacob, there were whites and Latinos and African Americans, and Jews and probably a Hari-Krishna or two, who knows. Why does it take devastation on such a monumental scale for us to get to a place of simple decency?

JACOB. Be happy for it. I remember walking through the rubble after we were liberated, and I was by the side of the road on my way to see Rokhol, our neighbor who had survived. And who knew how to find her- or how to reach her. All I knew was she was in Germany and that she had Sarah's diary, but this is another story. So there I was on a road in the middle of God knows where, and there were Poles and Russians and French and Americans, and everyone was trying to help each other. The Americans, my God, we were so happy to see them. I used to sell a great deal to the Americans. I was trading on the black market to survive- again, another story. And up walks to me this American, Abraham Goldrich, a private first class, and he knew I was a Jew, and he talked with me. He promised to send word to Brooklyn, he was from Flatbush, to my Aunt Hannah the only relative I had alive, and this is how I came to this country. Because Abraham Goldrich, this stranger, this brother, thousands of miles from his home, enlisted himself to track down my Aunt. This world has so many wonderful things and so many terrible...Where was I? Sometimes I forget...

ALAN. Do you ever wonder why we met?

JACOB. Who, you and I?

ALAN. Yes. I mean I could have easily said go away. Or you could have searched for a writer at Columbia or some other school. You have a hair here on the side of your nose. *(He gently removes the hair.)* There. Hell, you probably had gone to every other school. But these events, these momentary chance events, that can transform a life- being on the 99th floor of the Trade Center instead of the 98th-

JACOB. The man in front of me in line once. They shot him. Because he was taller then I, I suppose. Easier to reach. And I was on a train platform sick with fever and Benyamin, my friend from the shtetl tapped me on the shoulder. "Jakov, " he says "Jakov Fishkin. You survived! I know about your family. God rest their souls. But the diary. I know who has Sarah's diary. Now, what if I hadn't been on that platform?

ALAN. How do you make sense of that? The randomness…

KATE I think this has happened to me for a reason. My cancer. Wow, that is the first time that I said that. My cancer. Like- my purse. My shoes…My cancer.  I never thought in a million years that I'd be saying that….I have cancer. Anyway it's not like I ever had to fight any real battles. I've always been so lucky. My family always had enough money. I went to good schools. I had all the Beatles albums… So I can't help but believe I am being tested here, and I have to make the most of it.

ALAN. Only you could make cancer sound so positive-

DEB. She's a God, I'm telling you.

KATE Deb, don't you feel that way? When you got sick didn't you feel-

DEB. I was furious. Fucking furious. How dare they say I am going to die. I am nowhere near through living!

KATE. I feel blessed, honestly, I do. It all makes this weird kind of sense to me…

JAKOV. I like you much better when we are out of the ghetto. You are so different there.

*Jakov is sitting in some hay with Sarah. He is holding a jug.*

JAKOV. You laugh outside and walk as though you are about to run. There your face is always stern, and you stoop as though you are carrying too much flour.

JACOB. We had gone to find father again because there were stories that more Germans were hunting down Jews. But this time we had gotten very lost, and we were hiding in a barn and had stopped where the pigs were eating and drinking. I had found an old jug and because I was thirsty had been drinking. Sarah was sleeping, and she woke up and had caught me staring at her.

JAKOV. Do you remember the fire in the ghetto? As terrible as it was, I remember your face reflected in the flames. You looked so beautiful.

SARAH. Jakov, what is in that jug that you found?

JAKOV. Nothing. Just water.

JACOB. But I was not telling the truth. Some wine or liquor was left in it, and it was so sweet to taste.

JAKOV. Look, come here and look in the pig's water. See. Your eyes are as blue as Khane's, deep blue. And your hair is blonde like hers. Even Fanya is jealous of you. She wishes she was a scholar like you. This is why I enjoy your company. I feel safe and proud with you, my sister. I will cross bridges and travel through villages with you and never feel worried.

JACOB. She was resting her head on my shoulder. I will never forget.

SARAH. We may be forced to separate, dear brother. We must be prepared for that.

JAKOV. But how? *(They are looking in the water still and see the reflection of a very old woman.)* Do you see what I see? *(Sarah nods, and they turn around abruptly.)*

AN OLD WOMAN. Please do not be afraid. I'll not harm you. *(She has come up on them from behind.)* But I can tell you where you can find your father.

SARAH. Who are you?

AN OLD WOMAN. I am just an old farm woman, who feels for your people.

SARAH. Are you an angel?

JAKOV. Sent by God to help us find our father?

AN OLD WOMAN. *(Crossing herself)* I am no angel, dear Lord, no. I am older than any angel. But I have seen what is happening to your people. And I try to help. Whenever I can. I know your father and how good a man he is. You wait here, and I will tell him that you are on my farm. It is better that you stay here, I am not sure how close the police are.

JACOB. And she left, and Sarah and I both got nervous, so we hid in the hay in case she was lying.

SARAH. *(From in the hay, neither of them can be seen, only voices.)* Listen carefully. We must pray to God and believe in him. Never lose hope. When you despair, remember. Remember Fanya's beautiful face, and your so serious sister, and how we laughed and fought. Your little brother and sister, how much they adore you. Your mother and father and their love and devotion for you. Bobie when she smiles, and her wrinkles. The Germans they have deprived us of so much, but they will never be able to take away our memories. *(A beat, the pile of hay is quiet.)* Remember that always, alright?

JAKOV. *(From in the hay)* I will never forget.

JACOB. And when she came back, the old woman walked right up and began to talk to us as we hid. Knowing exactly where we were hiding and why, but never mentioning it.

AN OLD WOMAN. Your father is all right. I assured him that you were here and safe. He will wait until it gets dark and come for you. I will bring you food.

SARAH. *(Coming out from the hay)* You are so very kind. I think Jakov is asleep. He must be very tired.

 *The old woman finds the jug and smells it.*

SARAH. Thank you for helping us.

KATE. Doctor, thank you so much for seeing us so soon.

 *An examination room, Alan is with Kate and a doctor.*

DOCTOR. No need to thank me. We have all the test results, and there are many ways to treat this, but first if I may, please allow me to touch your chest.

KATE. Certainly.

JACOB. And as we waited, Sarah and the woman became good friends. And she took Sarah by the hand.

AN OLD WOMAN

*(Holding Sarah's hand.)* No need to thank me. But my dear child, I feel your worry through your veins, the roar of your blood rushing through you. In the pounding of your pulse I hear your screaming. I hear hell.

DOCTOR. You are very angry, aren't you? You carry a great deal of anger right here over your heart.

AN OLD WOMAN. I also feel heaven. How is that possible? Heaven and hell, at the same time? You called me an angel, but my child, it is you who are the angel. There is something you did not tell me, isn't there? Please, tell me.

DOCTOR. What are you angry about, do you know? Was there something that you might not even be aware that is upsetting you?

SARAH. I'm writing a diary. I enter everything I see and feel, and when I do that, I feel I am speaking to the future. And to God. I tell him how much I admire His creation. I also argue with him. Ask questions and demand answers, and when I do this, I feel so near to Him. I feel that I'm in Heaven. At times I fall asleep with my pen in hand, and then when I awake, I see Hell again.

KATE. I can never clean mirrors or windows to this day. I make someone else do it, ask Alan… My mother- she died just three weeks after I came to this country. She had a heart attack. And was gone before my father even came home. And I was here, thousands of miles from home… See, my family didn't want me to come here, to go to college, but I assured them it was just to go to school but that was a lie. I secretly knew I wanted to live here. It was my dream ever since I was five and bought my first box of Rice Krispies to come to America. And I remember how hard my mother cried at the airport- "you could still not go- there is work here, you could just not go." And it was so sad, but I remember feeling this is just why I have to go, so that I can do what I want to do and not what they will make me do. And the family was waving goodbye and the kids where jumping up and down, but she was still knocking on the plate of glass as I walked down the gate. She was sobbing and shaking her head no, no- and three weeks later I was back in that same airport for her funeral. She had been cooking dinner for the family, and they found her in the kitchen. No one said it was my fault- this was her second heart attack- but even the nieces and nephews were quiet as I walked back down from the gate to meet them. And I looked over at the plate of glass, and I could swear there were still handprints from where she had been banging…

AN OLD WOMAN. I would very much like to read this diary.

SARAH. I'd like you to, but you can't. It is in Yiddish.

AN OLD WOMAN. Then I can feel it. Touch it. I could rest my head upon it. I could bring it to my church and place it on the altar.  Could tell my priest and my congregation.

SARAH. Do you think you could care for it? Keep it safe and then give it back to me when I came for it?

AN OLD WOMAN. Of course, my dear. I would be honored.

DOCTOR. You have some important work to do with this loss, Kate.

KATE. But I thought I had.  I thought I had, you know, come to terms with it. It was years ago.

DOCTOR. She is holding onto you or you to her. I can feel that very clearly.

SARAH. Is it possible that I have found a home for my beloved diary? I must be dreaming.

AN OLD WOMAN. No, my child, you are definitely not dreaming. God, the Almighty, the compassionate, the merciful, heard your prayers and directed you to this barn. As he led Mother Mary to another barn to give birth to the Lord Jesus.

DOCTOR. It is no accident this is in your lung. Right over your heart. You must let go.

JACOB. I woke up and the old lady was laughing and caressing my hands.

AN OLD WOMAN. Come here, my little drunken friend.

JAKOV. What are you doing?

SARAH. She can tell us things, Jakov. About your future. She sees.


JACOB. Before I could say, "Sarah, you <u>are</u> crazy," the woman had grabbed my hand, and at first closed her eyes, but then she looked hard into mine.

AN OLD WOMAN. Young man, there are a lot difficult times ahead for you. You'll be very lonely and make a long and distant journey in search of happiness. I'm not sure what you will find. You will also suffer sickness and other disappointments, but you'll survive them. In the end, you'll emerge with some scars, but they too will heal.

DOCTOR. You have a great deal of work to do, but you will be fine. You'll be just fine. Do you believe me?

KATE. Yes.

JACOB. And just then my father arrived, and I jumped up and hugged him.

JAKOV. Taté, Taté! She said you would be all right!

DAVID. Dear woman, I do not know how to thank you.

DANTCHIKA. My name is Dantchika. You do not recognize me? I know I have aged.

JAKOV. She can tell the future, Father. Sarah, did she tell you yours?

JACOB. But Sarah said nothing.

DANTCHIKA. Remember my promise to you, Sarah. Bring me your diary, and I will watch over it.

DAVID. We need to get home now. Come on. While it is dark. There is a rumor the ghetto will be liquidated.

KATE. *(Putting on her clothes in the examining room)* What do you think?

ALAN. I want to believe him. I mean he spent a great deal of time with you and was very kind. Much more human than any of the other doctors. And Lord knows I'd like to believe in spiritual things and the power to heal. But I couldn't help but think-

KATE. He was telling me what I need to hear?

ALAN. Yes. And that was making him very powerful. Kind of hard not to pick him for a physician.

68

KATE. But he is still going to use chemo. He doesn't disregard the Western while he incorporates the Eastern. Look, if my choice is the compassionate possibly loopy physician or Dr. Chemo-by-the numbers, who shuffles papers while we discuss my dwindling life expectancy, I'll take the doctor who at least looks me in the eye.

SARAH. I liked her, Father.

JAKOV. She was very old. She may even be older than Bobie.

SARAH. How did she know you, Father?

DAVID. Dantshicka was a good friend of Bobie's. She even taught Bobie how to apply healing cups and which leaves are good for which ailments. But I never believed in these myths. She would look at your hand and predict your future, but she stopped doing that a long, long time ago.

SARAH. Why?

DAVID. She said that one had to accept the good and the bad in life, and everyone wanted to hear only the good. We youngsters used to call her "the witch." She left the shtetl when our Ghetto was set up. The Gentiles had to leave, so they were given other homes. But why are you bothering me with all this? We have more serious things to worry about than an old lady.

SARAH. Dantshika read my hand-

JAKOV. And mine too, Taté!

SARAH. I had such a strange feeling, Father. I started to tremble.

JAKOV. I didn't tremble. I didn't feel anything at all, just her wrinkly, dry, old hand.

SARAH. But so warm… It is bitter cold out, but her hands were warm as fire…

JACOB. Do you know I used to escape and come back?

ALAN. What?

ENSEMBLE. **Thursday, 19th March 1942 Today Finished Reading the Book "Crime and Punishment" Dostoyevsky.**

SARAH. The sun shines in on us in our prison. It penetrates our iron gratings and beams down as if to say, "Rejoice in the light I bring you. See: I do not avoid stealing in here in my effort to quiet your exasperated, aching hearts! Delight in my splendor and brilliance! Hope that these, my rays, thrown from afar, will bring you true joy!"

JACOB. I used to escape from the labor camp. Sarah would help me. I used to duck under the wire- there are some benefits to being this small, and I would go out into the fields. I even made a friend there. Yurek. He was my age, a shepherd boy. I told him my name was Yanek. I was with Gentiles. You see, among the Gentiles, one used their Polish name, but this –

ALAN and JACOB. Is another story.

JACOB. Yes. And I taught him many things: how to make a bow and arrow, to carve a whistle for his sheep and cows. He brought me to his father.

*The verse form is used again, to honor the original text used*

YUREK
This is my friend Yanek.
He helps gather the sheep
And the cows.
He can even speak to them.

YUREK'S FATHER
*(After a long stare)* Come, let's eat now.

YUREK
May I introduce my new friend to my other ones?

YUREK'S FATHER
Today Yanek must go home
He doesn't live far. He'll ask his parents
Whether you may take him home with you.
In the meantime, don't tell your friends about
Him.
They don't need to know what you have in mind.

YUREK
I won't tell anyone.
But may he come again tomorrow?

YUREK'S FATHER
Yes, he may meet you

Out in the field at any time,
And you may do anything
Both of you would like to do.

JACOB. And that kind man, I will never forget him; he gave me food to take
back, and I smuggled it in. This helped my family to remain alive, this food.

ALAN. This is amazing. You were actually free?

JACOB. I suppose so, but at the time, I was just going to meet Yanek. It was
a lovely hillside, not even a kilometer from our camp. I taught him many
things, and he showed me how to milk a cow. You have never tasted milk
such as this… My God, to think of it. Even now I can taste it… Anyway I
used to come back crawling with the food tied to my legs but so happy to
have been in the fields. And Sarah would meet me at the wire. Until one day
she wasn't there, she was late.

SARAH.
Yankele, dear little brother, forgive me
I was talking with people. People who knew our shtetl.

JAKOV.
Let's go back to Rubzewitz.
We'll get the little ones out
Of Ivenietz and all of us—
Father, Mother, you, I, and Grandmother
Will go to the good Gentiles
And find a place among them.

SARAH.
I must tell you a secret, but you must promise
Not to tell Mother and Father.
The seven hundred young children
Were taken out of the ghetto
And murdered in a horrible way.
Our Itshele and Mirele were among them.
And that is not the entire tragedy.
The elderly who remained in Rubzewitz
Were driven out to pits and murdered.
Only with the Gentiles's help could the German's perpetrated this
Slaughter.

Dear little brother, there is no reason
To go back to Rubzewitz.
The Gentiles will not accept us
And we won't have refuge among them.

Do you hear what I'm saying?
Do you understand my words?

JACOB. But all I could say was:

JAKOV.
Do you know what you are saying?
How can you invent such stories?
Have you gone mad?

JACOB. My viciousness sent her off in tears, but how could I accept it?
How does one accept such things. I remember lying awake at night seeing
my Bobie falling into that pit over and over. Trying to scream but we could
not hear… She had lost her mind, my sister. I would find a way to escape
from that place, or I too would go mad…

ALAN. But you did escape. Every day.

JACOB. But there was always the food.

ALAN. You never thought just once, "Here I am in the fields, free, let me
just run away."

JACOB. And leave them with no food? My family needed the food. No, this
was unthinkable…And then soon after Sarah came with an announcement
that the Germans needed men to mend boots and sew gloves. They would
send tradesmen to Smolensk to work in factories. This could possibly save
some of our lives. She said that the elders thought Father should go.

SARAH. You'll take care of Father and
I'll do the same here for Mother.

JACOB. Mother had only gotten worse since we left our shtetl. She often sat
for hours, so still, weak with fever.

*Shoshke is seen in another light sitting very still.*

JAKOV.
How can you say you'll separate from Father
And I from Mother? And how will she
Survive without her children?
And without her beloved husband?

SHOSHKE
Oh, take not from me my silvery dream,
But let me drown in its gleam.
I've tasted no joy in reality—
In dreams let forgetfulness come to me.


*David joins her, and he and Shoshke begin to dance together very
closely as she continues speaking softly and passionately:*

SHOSHKE
Oh, let me spin out my fancies of silver!
In dreams let my spirit run free.
With no space in my life for my desire—


*Shoshke and David are about to kiss and Sarah speaks the last line
with Shoshske:*

SARAH and SHOSHSKE
At least let me dream and, dreaming, expire.

DAVID. *(Stops and turns sharply to Sarah.)* How do you know that poem?


*He and Sarah and Jakov are back in the woods, years earlier,
coming home from rescuing Sarah.*

DAVID. Where did you hear it? Did you read it?

SARAH. Why?

DAVID. That is the poem your mother used to recite-

SARAH. Really? Tell me about her, Father. Tell me about Shoshke.

JAKOV. There you go again. Pappa, I worry about her. *(To Sarah.)* She is
your mother. And mine. And she cries a lot, and gives all our food to the
people of Koydanov.

DAVID. That isn't all, Yankele. Your mother was- is- someone indescribably
special.

JACOB. I had never heard my father talk of my mother. You see, in those days mother was mother and father was father, and if they gave each other a kiss, this was on a holiday. Nowadays? My God, the carrying on-

ALAN. But that is another story.

JACOB. It is a good story, too, believe me… Anyway, we stopped and sat down, and Taté talked of traveling to Minsk with our Zeyde. Now, Minsk, this was the big city, and soon he was introduced to a group of young people, part of a group called Bundistn. See, everyone in these days was political- this was the time of great ideas and great struggles. Do you know of this Bund? No, why do I even ask… This is a very powerful Jewish organization to this day, but back then, the Bundistn believed a new socialist order was the answer. You see, you had the Zionists who wished for a Jewish state in Palestine- my Taté, was one of these- and you had the Bund.

DAVID. There were hundreds of people. And I pushed to get a view of what was going on. Then a man got up and introduced:

SPEAKER. From Kharkov, a long way from Minsk, a seamstress. The leader of the Bund movement from the Kharkov region: Sonia Galperin!

*Shoshke is bathed in light now about to recite a poem.*

DAVID. And I have never seen such hair, such rich chestnut hair, and eyes like the ocean, and cheekbones that seemed to rest atop her sweet smile. And I have never heard such applause. And then her smile faded, and she began:

SHOSHKE *(This time as though about all peoples)*
Oh, take not from me my silvery dream.
But let me drown my sorrows in its gleam.

DAVID. Now I have heard my share of speakers since, but your mother…

SHOSHKE
I've tasted no joy in reality—
In dreams, then let forgetfulness come to me.

JAKOV. Mother, what?

DAVID. There is a story about a well-known entertainer and a rabbi. Now the chairman introduces this great entertainer who steps forward and recites:

Chapter ten verse five. The Shepherd… And when he finishes there is much applause and bravos. And then the Rebbe is introduced, modestly attired, shabby beard, and says, "Ladies and gentleman, if I may recite Chapter ten, verse five, The Shepherd"…And at the end of his delivery, there was no thundering applause, no standing ovation. Instead, all present were speechless and crying. The chairman approaches the entertainer, "Tell me please," he says, "both of you used the same text. Why was there such a marked difference in the reaction of the audience?" "It's easy," replied the entertainer, "I know the verse well, but he, he knows the shepherd."

SHOSHKE
Oh, let me spin out my fancies of silver!
In dreams let my spirit run free.
With no space in my life for desire—
At least let me dream and dreaming, expire!


*Back in the labor camp.*


SARAH.
You must understand:
It is our situation that forces us to participate
In these activities. Perhaps this is the <u>only way</u> that
At least one of us will remain alive.
If we stay together, we'll perish together.
We can't go home and there is nowhere to hide.

JACOB. And this made her cry again. But this time I knew she was right.

JAKOV. Ssh! Ssh! Don't cry. I'll go to Smolensk with Father.

JACOB. But there was no guarantee we would be allowed to go. The news about Smolensk spread like wildfire about the camp and all that were able hoped to be asked. To be somewhere other than where we were… And mother neither cried nor asked questions. She just kept shaking her head.

SARAH. Do you hear what I am saying, Mother?

SHOSHKE. I hear what you are saying,  Child.

SARAH.
If you don't want them to
They won't go to Smolensk
The Germans aren't forcing us to do it.
Novick, the president of all the Jews here,
Has important connections.

He puts great trust in me and advised me
That this is the only way to remain alive.

SHOSHKE.
What can my life be like
When my soul is taken from me?

JACOB. And she clutched my Father and me and held us tight.

SARAH.
In our Torah it is written
That God will curse His people
He will punish us for our sins
And we shall suffer hail and brimstone.

It is written that one from each city
And two from each family will survive.
Our wise men taught
That we are not to question God's ways,
But we shall all ask that he keep His word
And that, if not two, than at least one
From our family will survive.

JACOB.
And then slowly… Mother let go of us.
Trucks were ready to transport us.
My father's name was called. *(A guard does this: "Da-vid Fishkin".)*
And immediately after, mine. *(Again the guard, "JAKOV. Fishkin".)*
Sarah wiped the tears from her face.
Mother stood motionless.
Father and I boarded a truck
and we took our last look at Sarah and Mother.

*Jacob takes a long deep breath and swallows some water.*

**End of Act Two**

# ACT THREE

*Jacob is talking, and as he does, Sarah and Shoshke are seen from far away and they seem to disappear.*

JACOB. They drove us for days, herding us overnight into ruined synagogues. Then back into the trucks again. And then trains… My whole life has been one long journey, a constant traveling, always away, further and further away from that point, that one moment in time. They get smaller and smaller, my mother… and Sarah.


ENSEMBLE. **Wednesday, 29th April 1942. It Snowed This Afternoon.**

SARAH. Every blade of grass has a mother, every leaf is cradled in the airy arms of the wind, but no grass and no leaf is ever cuddled as long against warm mother's breast as is the deep shadow-filled green of the woods in that Eastern land, our land, where the hot sunbeams shine down. There people live free and, perhaps, happily even now. There the wide salt seas penetrate the fertile black fields, there the budding fruit glistens before one's eye, there the lovely, golden sheaves change color as one looks at them and bring joy and happiness and nourishment and fill one with such pride of life. It begins to snow, and it seems that before long there will be white everywhere and winter will return with its cold and dampness. However, the snow soon stops and the remaining patches of white melt. The warmth returns and the sky is cleared of clouds. Melancholy evening comes, bringing with it quiet and loneliness. There is nothing to do, so one goes to bed.

*Alan and his wife are in their bathroom. He begins to shave her head.*

KATE. Alan. Please, let me-

ALAN. No, come on. This is the one haircut I can give you. You are not going to take away my joy here.

KATE. There's a word for men like you-

ALAN. What? That want to help?

KATE. That like to shave their wives bald.

ALAN. Really?

KATE. Their heads, Jerk. Shave their heads…. God, it was really falling out, wasn't it?

ALAN. Who cares…

KATE. Do you like my wig?

ALAN. Very much.

KATE. I love the color. It's like an orangutan red.

ALAN. Not sure Revlon calls it that…

KATE. Well, why not? I think I'll get another one. Long and blonde. For my ever changing moods. *(She is bald now.)* Christ, look at me… I look….so….Well, it's not that terrible, is it?

ALAN. I kind of like it.

KATE. You know I really don't want to die.

ALAN. Stop! Of course not.

KATE. No, I mean I really don't. So, I don't plan on doing it, okay?

ALAN. Okay by me.

KATE. You missed a spot here. *(She reaches for the clippers.)*

ALAN. Sorry.  *(She gives them back.)* What?

KATE. Well, go on, finish, will you? Nothing worse than a man who can't finish what he started…

JACOB. I have a funny story for you.

> *Jacob is talking to Alan who continues to shave Kate's hair. Both realities are happening.*

ALAN. Go on.

JACOB. When I was finally coming here to America. My God, what a day that was…

ALAN. You must have been so happy.

JACOB. Well, actually I was sad. And scared. I was all alone you see. All my relatives except my Aunt here in Brooklyn- so few that I knew were even alive. My neighbor Rokhol, who found Sarah's diary, but other than this I was alone, alone in all the world. And I was just a boy remember, seventeen, and sailing all by myself to this great big country, and I did not like the ocean, or rather, it did not like me. I got so seasick. So there I was barely able to step off the gangplank I was so weak in the knees, and everyone else was hugging each other and kissing, so glad to be back in each other's arms. And I remember it was Rosh Hashanah, the New Year, and the holidays were always the most difficult time, and all of a sudden, I got such a flush of joy and my heart started to race. I knew I would be all right in this land, and you know what did this to me? I looked up, and there was this great big balloon in the sky, huge and it had written on it "Good Year." And I thought these Americans, they know how to celebrate the High Holy Days!

ALAN. That's so funny!

JACOB. I'm going to like it here in America.

SARAH. We do not deserve to be free, for we did not before this understand how to conduct ourselves. And it is for that we are suffering now, not for nothing.

ENSEMBLE. **Saturday, 11th April 1942.**

SARAH. But the liberation of mankind cannot come through war, only through education. When the human mind has properly developed, all evil will, as a matter of course, disappear by itself. Knowledge is the salvation of humankind, which is why everyone should dedicate himself to it. It is not the systems which are good or bad, but people—people alone. And there is no such thing as good or evil; there is knowledge and ignorance. Every person with knowledge is, ipso facto, for that reason alone, a noble individual. He may on occasion do something harmful out of necessity but not out of malice.

JACOB. Years later, I opened my own business on Kings Highway. Stylish Shoes, for plus sizes. I learned this trade from a man, Danny Lombardi, who had a few shops in Brooklyn-Widestyles. Maybe you've heard of them? Now I was grateful to this man for giving me this chance, but I made the most of it myself, you see, and I helped make his business very profitable. My customers all came to me because they trusted me. And I knew a good shoe.

DAVID. Now, all of you, watch my little Yankele. You must learn how to cut the shoe along the pattern like so. No, Rabbi, use this side of the blade. This is the dull side…Yankele will show you while I help the butcher over here. And the violin player. How can I possibly teach you all to cobble at once… Doesn't anyone here actually know how to make a shoe? Well then, we must learn quickly.

SARAH. Yes, education! But not in the sense of creating ever larger and more powerful machines for the destruction of people so that a greater number will fall by a single shot, and more of them drop for no reason at all. No! People should not educate themselves in that manner or with those goals but to learn to ease human suffering, to create much that is good, and to put a stop to wrong living.

JACOB. So after a few years of hard work, I came to this Mr. Lombardi, and I asked him if I could have a percentage, a partnership which I offered to pay for, instead of wages and a small commission since I was ordering most of the styles, and at least two-thirds of the customers I knew by name. And he refused, so I walked out, and a few month later, I opened my own shop. On the other side of town because I didn't want to seem ungrateful, and do you know what this man did? He bought the shop next to me and opened up another one of his stores to try to put me out of business. But my customers liked my shoes, and his store was losing money, and one day he walked up to me sweeping outside my shop, and I said "Good morning, Mr. Lombardi." And he said "Good morning, Fishkin." And then he said "You know, they got six million of you Jews, why couldn't they have gotten six million and one."

SARAH. At present, of course, this is but a thought. It does not happen just because a person thinks that way. That does not create it. Many more people will yet fall in the struggle to establish the world and humanity upon a truly good foundation, many waters will yet flow by. But in the course of an extended period, the world will indeed structure itself as people determined dozens of years earlier. True, we shall no longer be here by that time, but people will be happy. The old ways of life will be discontinued, and Humankind's wild, brutal emotions curbed. New thinkers and lovers of life will come forth, teaching that good is not only for the chosen but for all humanity.

JACOB. Do you know why I come here so often?

ALAN. You like the water?

JACOB. Yes, this and I love being in this school. This university. September 1941 was a particularly sad time. When the schools opened this year, the Jewish children were forbidden to attend. I longed for my teachers and the classes every day. As the weeks passed, they ordered us to come to our school and chop wood to make fires. We passed through the front door where a sign hung: Jews and Dogs Not Allowed. I was preparing the kindling as I did at home when I heard the bell ring, and I cannot tell you why I thought I should, but I put down my hatchet and joined the children outside. To my surprise, no one paid any attention to me, so I joined the students when they went back in the class. Now the teacher, Stozipiczowa, recognized me, but she did not stop me.

STOZIPICZOWA. Hello, Yanek, you will need these.

JACOB. And she gave me paper and a pencil and some books. And later on before the end of the class she gave me a note labeled "For This Afternoon" and it said, "Do the same thing you did before." *(A bell rings)* So I went back to work and told my foreman, and he said that he would cover for me. So that afternoon, I played outside and then went to class, and it was Mr. Stozipicz, her husband, who often drank too much, but was a master teacher of arithmetic.

STOZIPICZ. Mr. Yanek, please take your seat. *(nervously)* Would everyone please begin the problem on the board. *(As the children begin working, he takes a sip of something from a mug, he then walks past JAKOV.'s desk)* Very good, Yanek. *(then whispers)* Next period, continue to do the same thing. *(The bell rings.)*

JACOB. As the bell rang, I ran to my group. The foreman was waiting and instructed the others to pay no attention and shoved me back onto the playground. The third session was my favorite, Natural Science with Mr. Schultz.

MR SCHULTZ. Please everyone, everyone, take your seats. We have a lot to cover today. *(He hands JAKOV. a sandwich.)* I believe you left this in your last class, Yanek. You must be more careful. Now class, let us begin. Who knows the difference between mammals and reptiles?

JACOB. I will never forget that day in school. I rushed back the next day to chop wood, but the foreman forbid me to try again. He said nothing more. But I saw that his hands were shaking, and he would not look me in the eye. The next day there was a new foreman. Weeks later, I was in the school basement and Stozipiczowa came down and motioned me to sit with her.

STOZIPICZOWA. How are you, Yakov? I know, you needn't answer. All of the teachers miss you. We would like to help, but it could be very dangerous for us. Anyway, I've brought you some books. Take them home and see what you can do with them.

*The bell rings.*

JAKOV. You'll be late.

STOZIPICZOWA. Yes…

*She goes. And Yakov sits and looks at the book.*

JACOB. I never in my life attended another class after that one day. Ever. But I have had many teachers. My father, Sarah certainly, and there were many Rabbis. *He takes a sip of water.* Not bad. But there was never anyone quite like Reb Chayim.

REB. How many Rabbis does it take to make a decent pair of shoes? You, David and you, little Yankele, why can I not have more like you?

JACOB. Reb Chayim was our foreman at Smolensk; he ran our workshop. The former manager of a large German shoe factory was our commandant. We were very lucky- he was not cruel and he respected Reb Chayim. Everyone respected Reb Chayim. He once asked Reb Chayim why there were so few Jewish artisans and he replied:

REB. I will make artisans out of them all.

JACOB. Now to reach the attic where we slept was a very tall ladder, and the rungs of this ladder would break from so many having to use it. It was Reb Chayim who had the idea-

REB. Don't do that. You will just fall, and then you will have nothing but broken bones to make shoes with. Here, take these new rungs and put them in, like so. There you see? What are you doing?

JAKOV. They are broken. I am throwing them away.

REB. No. No, you are not. Nothing is to be thrown away. Is your name not Jacob? If there is one thing that a Jacob should know it is about ladders.

JACOB. And then once we had all climbed up to the attic-

REB. I, for one, do not want to be disturbed every night, do you?

JACOB. He would take the ladder and replace the new rungs with the broken rungs so that it was all but impossible to climb again, and the Guards would leave us alone. And that attic in the night, it was our- our fortress.

JAKOV. I stole some socks, Reb Chayim. From the German's laundry. They are much warmer. I gave them to my Taté, but he would only take one. I want you to have the other.

REB. You keep them, Yankele. What good is one warm foot?

JAKOV. You can alternate. Like we do.

REB. If you get another pair they can be mine.

JACOB. He taught those that had no trade to be craftsmen and saved their lives. And we'd take the newspapers, we'd smuggle from the wrapped vegetables, and he would read them, and it was like the newsreels at the cinema-

REB. *(like an announcer)* You are listening to the Voice of Smolensk…."Yes," report the Germans, "the Bolsheviks will die of starvation like frozen dogs. Moscow will no longer be the capital and the Volga will not be the boundary. Fierce battle are raging in the vicinity of Stalingrad. Leningrad is surrounded."

JACOB. And as always he would burn the paper with a small candle so the Germans would not know.

REB. This is not news; this is propaganda. Do not be worried, my friends, my comrades. The Russians will be here very soon. Tomorrow will be here before you know it. I fought in the Polish Army. I fought against these Russians, and I promise you they can fight. You see this knee, I was shot down and still can't kick with this knee because of those frozen dogs. You want to see frozen dogs, I'll show you frozen dogs. How are my sweethearts tonight? *(Reb Chayim starts to howl softly and from below three dogs join in singing.)*

JACOB. There were three vicious guard dogs that were let out into the workroom at night to keep us in the attic. And Reb Chayim had sung so many times to them that they had become used to his voice and would no longer bark. Instead, they would sing along with him.

*He sings again, and the dogs howl softly along with him.*

REB. You see, Yankele, the dogs don't want to bite; they must be taught to attack. Only the Germans want to attack. The dogs only do as we do, as they are told. And there they must sit in the cold as we do all night.

ALAN. Jacob, I've been dying to ask you: What do you think about yesterday?

JACOB. Yesterday?

ALAN. We are at war now. We started bombing in Afghanistan.

JACOB. Did we?

JAKOV. How come the dogs listen to you Reb Chayim?

REB. Because I listen to them.

JAKOV. But they are just barking and howling…

REB. No, you must listen. Even this barking is for a reason. All language,
birds, dogs, is for a reason…You must learn to listen. To interpret. My gift is
I can hear dogs. You see the little one on the end?  She is always hungry
because she is so small. That is why she will bite you first. The fat one in the
middle, he is old and hard of hearing. This is why he sings the loudest. But it
is the one there, farthest away from us, that you must watch very carefully.
Even she doesn't trust me. She only barks if the other two are barking.
Otherwise she just shows her teeth…My dog at home, Hava, she loved to
talk…We would go for long walks in the woods and talk for hours. Wait,
ssh, do you hear?

JAKOV. I only hear your dogs howling and…the wind…

REB. This is because you do not listen. Close your eyes. If I show you a
picture you look at it, no? What do you see? No, do not just look at who and
what is in the picture. Look at the whole picture, at everything, the colors,
how it is arranged, look into the faces and past the faces. Now you begin to
hear. No?

> *The sound of airplanes approaching is heard. It should get louder
> and louder and then bombing begins. There are sirens.*

JAKOV. It's the Russians! The planes are coming! Taté, the planes!

JACOB. And we'd all rush to that attic window and look out, and the sky
would fill. One by one until it was black with locusts. And then the
fireworks, and we would sing. Reb Chayim would lead us all in song, and
the bombs would explode, and the dogs would bark and bark, and we prayed
that the Russian would destroy them all.

> *Everyone is singing loudly:*

Koy amor, omar has-shem: zokarti lokh khesed ne-u-ray-ikh
Ahavas klu-lo-soy-ikh, ahavas klu-lo-soy-ikh,
Lekhtekh akharay, akharay bamidbor, be-eretz loy zoruah.

(So saith the Lord: I remember the grace of youth
The love of your nuptials, yea the love of your nuptials
When you followed me, followed me in the desert, in a land unsown.)

ALAN. But that was so different. That whole war was different.

JACOB. Maybe. But the bombs were still bombs, dropping all around and
we still sang. Sometimes even those that the bombs drop on are singing. We
could have been killed, but at least it was not by Hitler…

DEB. I mean I marched all through the sixties, Alan, don't get me wrong.
I've fasted against capitol punishment. But after those towers fell, I said "get
the fucker," I did. My first reaction was "bomb the fucker off the face of the
earth…"

ALAN. The Good War. That's what they called it. And I used to laugh at that
anachronism…

DEB. Paradox-

ALAN. Whatever. I'd say no! It's like that scene in Monty Python and the
Holy Grail- you fight me and cut off my arm and I cut off yours- you cut off
my leg and whack- off goes yours. And pretty soon we are both rolling
around in the mud with no arms and legs.

DEB. Alan, I hate to tell you but in that scene only one knight gets his arms
and legs whacked off. There's only one knight bobbling around bleeding to
death and the other one rides away.

GERMAN COMMANDER. Ich bin der neue Aufseher auf die
Schuhwerke!!!

JACOB. I am the new over-seer of the shoe factory- these were the first
words our new commandant said. The war front was changing, and our old
tolerant commander was gone. And this new dimwit ordered Reb Chayim
down from the attic!

GERMAN COMMANDER. Schnell! Schnell!

JACOB. And Reb Chayim fell while trying to climb the broken ladder and
picked himself up but was limping badly. The commander searched him and

found the newly carved rungs of the ladder. He gave them back to Reb Chayim

GERMAN COMMANDER. I believe these are yours.

JACOB. And they marched him out, *(Reb Chayim exits)* and we never saw him again. He was maybe… thirty-five. The commandant ordered the rest of us down from the attic, and many fell and were hurt, and then we were searched.

SOLDIER. Herr Commandant!

JACOB. They had found the pair of socks that I had stolen for Reb Chayim. *(The commander nods his head.)* And I was immediately taken outside and beaten in front of my father and the entire barracks.

> *The soldier begins to whip Jakov.*

JACOB. This was not the first time I had been whipped; they once beat us back in the ghetto by the side of the road for not working hard enough, and many, many were killed. I had run away then, but this time there was no escape, and I was terrified. But you see, God was with me that day because after the first few lashes, I did not feel anything.

> *Jakov is running and finds himself in the woods. It is months earlier and he is alone. He falls to the ground and a man comes from out of the darkness behind him.*

TALL PARTISAN. Jakov?

JAKOV. I'm sorry, I did not mean to run. I will work much harder.

TALL PARTISAN. It is Hershal. From Koydanov.

JAKOV. What are you doing here?

TALL PARTISAN. What are you?

JAKOV. They beat us, and I ran. I am so happy to see you.

TALL PARTISAN. Don't worry, I watch over you. All of the time.

JAKOV. You do?

TALL PARTISAN. This is our job, no?  We are good at hiding. I have even been to your house.

JAKOV. When?

TALL PARTISAN. I look in from time to time. Your windows.

JAKOV. Why don't you tell me? Why don't you come inside?

TALL PARTISAN. It is not good for too many to see us. Though your sister has seen me.

> *Sarah appears at a windowsill.*

SARAH. Who's there? Is there someone out there?

TALL PARTISAN. But our eyes met, and I ducked back into the forest.

JAKOV. Sarah?

TALL PARTISAN. You have to go back now. While you still have the strength. But don't worry. I watch over her. And your family. Now go, you know the way. *(He helps Jakov to leave.)*

> *Sarah is still at the window.*

ENSEMBLE. **Thursday, May 14th 1942.**

SARAH. I should like to find a person who would be in harmony with my character and my feelings. One from whom also I should be able to learn so much that is worthwhile.

ALAN. Her last entry in the diary is the only time she mentions love. Romantic love. I was so moved by that. She longed for someone…

JACOB. I was in love with a girl in our shtetl, but I was too young to even know. Her name was Fanya, and we used to fight and fight and roll on the ground and then hug and then fight some more. She was very beautiful. When I fell down a crawlspace looking for potatoes and into some rags at the camp and I was suffocating and they left me to die, it was Fanya who came to me and told me to climb to safety. I could see her though it was quite dark.

*Fanya appears in a pool of light.*

FANYA. Hello, Jakov. You look well.

JAKOV. As do you. These are sad times, but seeing you… I feel so much is possible.

FANYA. It may be, Jakov. It may be.

JACOB. After I was liberated and after Sarah's diary was returned to me, Rohkol told me Fanya lived nearby. I couldn't believe this…Fanya was alive. So I had a haircut and a shave, and I went to see her.

FANYA. Will you come to my wedding? My fiancé and I would be so honored.

JAKOV. Of course. So, you are to be married? Mazel Tov.

FANYA. Thank you…He has kind eyes like you, dear Yankele. You see there is much that is possible…

SARAH. Sometimes, however, the youthful heart asks no questions and refuses to stop and consider, does not care to know whether his character is good or bad but sees only the handsome exterior from which is so dazzling; one is oblivious of everything except the pleasure of being with him.

JACOB. Sarah did not try to escape, you know. Mother had already died. From typhus and hunger. And when the word came that the Germans were coming to liquidate the camp, Rohkol and her family, at least a hundred others took refuge in a hiding place in the wall. And they all hid and then escaped and this is how Rohkol found the diary. Years later because they hid in a wall and the Germans and the dogs did not sniff them out. Now, why is that, if not the Lord? And Rhokol begged Sarah to come, begged her to hide, and she said no. She was a Jew, and she would stay with the other Jews, and if it had come to this, she would die with her people…She refused to hide.

*The ensemble begins to pack themselves close together and form a living sculpture, the hiding Jews, as Sarah speaks*

SARAH. Yes, love and youth are two themes which contain much that is hidden, which combine and go together, two happy stages in life. One cannot forget them as long as one lives, and it is all very beautiful but not for us to think about, much less describe at this time, for it simply creates more pain when we probe into and concentrate on portraying it. Therefore, I shall not do so now. Let things continue to go as they are going so that I am not perturbed by questioning thoughts, for I feel that would cause me much pain and suffering…

JACOB. So though I didn't know it, all that was left of my family was my father and me, and he was getting weak and his legs and stomach were swelling. But we kept taking turns keeping each other alive. Trying to cheer each other up. Planning. They moved us by freight train from Smolensk to a series of camps as the front lines kept changing. The entire camp was herded into cars, and we had no idea where we were going.

*The ensemble is no longer the Jews in hiding, but the transport train packed with sick and hungry. This must not be literal at all but a stage picture or dance like movement.*

MOTL. We must get out of here.

LEYZER. We can cut the wires in the windows.

DAVID. I will help you. I am too weak to escape, but I can help.

MOTL. If some make it out, there will be more air for others.

LEYZER. If we don't, we will all suffocate.

JACOB. The bodies of the dead were piled up, and then those who could, stood on them to climb to the windows, and with rags rapped around their hands, pulled at the wires until they broke free.

ARIEH. My dear Jews, I was in the army, and we jumped from planes- listen to me. To begin with you must jump out feet first. You must hold on to the window with all your might until you feel both your feet touching the side of the car. Then you must push away from the car with your hands and feet, with all of your might. The wind will help you pull away from the moving train. You must not try to land on your feet. When you start falling, put your head between your legs as soon as you can.

JACOB. And then to demonstrate, he climbed out of the window and jumped.

*He does. The others try to help David, but he can't jump.*

DAVID. Please go, I can't.

MOTL. What about JAKOV.?

DAVID. Yes. Now, Yankele, you must go-

JAKOV. No. I am staying with you!

DAVID. You must go now, before it is too late.

JAKOV. I am to look after you. I promised Sarah. That was the plan! I am staying!

JACOB. And the others jumped from the train. I have no idea to this day if they survived. My father would not speak to me. For the first time he was angry. But when the train pulled in, we saw two large chimneys burning. This was in Plashov.

GUARDS. Macht schell! Macht schnell!

JACOB. We were being unloaded and told that the Germans needed some workers to fix their trucks. The smokestacks were part of the factory. Everyone was rushing off the trains- there was little time to think. Some of my cousins got in line and marched toward the factory, but my father grabbed me firmly by the hand. The rest of us were told to get back onboard, and my father pushed me back onto the train, and I kept asking why? Why? Somehow he knew. We arrived at a camp Blizhin, and by this time my father was very weak. I knew I had to get him food. I was very good at sneaking around, and after a few days, I found where the potatoes were stored and had managed to hide two or three and make my way back to the barracks.

RONTSHKA. You, Halt! Halt right there.

JACOB. This was the meanest of the Kapos that policed us. Kapos were chosen for the job because they were more brutal than the other guards. He had one hand amputated, and he wore a black glove. That is why we called him Rontshka, the hand. The day before, I had seen him shoot a man because he was too weak to get out of bed when his name was called.

RONTSHKA. Where are you going?

JACOB. Now I was already very weak, could barely walk in a straight line, and I knew he could smell blood.

RONTSHKA. Why are you shaking? Are you hiding something? Do I make you nervous?

JACOB. I was looking down at the ground, but I felt the strength of Sarah and my little brother and sister helping me. They willed me to slowly raise my head and look him squarely in the eyes, and I walked in a straight line

90

right past him and said, "I have no potatoes!" and saluted him as if he were my king. And he saluted me back. And then laughed and walked away. And I ran to Pappa.

DAVID. Where were you? We've been looking all over for you!

JACOB. And the whole barracks was there. And a Rabbi, Reb Moyshe stepped forward.

REB MOYSHE This is a very holy day, for today we celebrate the bar mitzvah of Jakov Fiskin.

JACOB. I had forgotten it was my birthday. And they brought forth a small Torah. And after I recited and sang my Haftorah, the men placed me on their shoulders, and we danced until our lookout yelled:

LOOKOUT. Be quiet! Now!

JACOB. And we all dove into our beds, and the lights were put out. But all through the night, one by one, I was congratulated. One does not ever forget such a Bar Mitvah…

DEB. Hey, how is she doing?

ALAN. I don't know.  It's only been an hour. Thanks for coming.

DEB. Not at all, gives me a chance to spend some quality time in the desperate and Spartan confines of a hospital waiting room. I actually am attracted to waiting rooms, did I ever tell you that? They are full of purpose-people's fate hang in the balance, like courtrooms and jury rooms. I love those. I like a place with purpose built in. Is this helping?

ALAN. Not at all.

DEB. Why I'm here…Your whole life is a waiting room, think about it. It's just that not every day the stakes are so clear.

ALAN. Thank God.

DEB. Oh, so are we believing these days?

ALAN. I believe there is too much beauty in living.

SARAH. I think how fortunate I am that God granted me the desire to do this, endowed me with love for pen and the ability to express everything in writing.

DEB. I brought a few folks with me if you don't mind.

> *The entire ensemble of actors joins Deb and Alan in the waiting
> room and they sit together and after a few hellos and thank yous,
> just sit quietly together, some reading.*

SARAH. In the quiet, illumined hours when I sit writing, spending time with
you, sharing all with you, you remain silent and locked away to all others.
You exist for me alone, you are joined to me only. Only for me do you live,
and me do you serve. And the same is true of me with regard to you, my
pen. I alone accumulate true materials to describe, characterize and
formulate for you, and I gather together the thoughts that sometimes burden
me and will not go away.

> *The ensemble has moved into a circle as if around a table.
> Rohkol stands. Jakov sits at the head of the table. An empty
> chair is next to him.*

ROHKOL. We have a very special guest with us for sedar this year, Jakov
Fishkin, our dear neighbor from Rubiezewicze, whose presence here this
evening brings us joy beyond words. And rather than have an empty chair
for the prophet Elijah, we all thought that the seat should be held for his
beloved sister, Sarah, whose diary is there in her place instead of the
Haggadah.

> *Jakov picks up the diary and holds it to his chest and begins to
> weep.*

ROHKOL. Why is this night different from all other nights…

SARAH. I did not think, last Sabbath day, that we would still be alive today
or that I would still be writing. I now consider myself fortunate just to have
lived through another day and to be able to listen to the beat of my heart and
pulse.

> *Alan is alone now in the waiting room. He is reading from the
> notebook of Sarah's writing. Two scenes are happening
> simultaneously, both with only one foot or one toe in reality.
> Kate appears looking into a large pane of mirror that is
> invisible and after a beat Sarah appears on the other side.
> Meanwhile a simple old man sits down in the waiting room
> next to Alan.*

KATE. *(to herself)* Look at my hands…

OLD MAN. Can I have that Tttt-time magazine, please.

ALAN. Sure. These suicide bombings are terrible, aren't they? There'll never be peace now.

KATE. Oh please, go away.

SARAH. Are you speaking to me or the pain in your fingers?

OLD MAN. The ss-saddest thing is this is nothing new. Ccc-centuries ago there was kkk-killing. And then there were periods where the swords were pp-put away.

KATE. I don't see you. Forgive me. But I don't want to. This is silly. Alan thinks it is so theatrical. I think it is a violation. I never wanted to even be in this play in the first place.

SARAH. You sound like my brother Jakov.

KATE. Your brother is the whole problem. He's the reason that my husband has gone crazy…

ALAN. My name is Alan, Alan Klutzenberg.

OLD MAN. And mm-mine is Moses. Kk-klutzenberg, this is-

ALAN. A burden. My whole life. Thanks, Dad.

OLD MAN. Oh, I know all about bb-burdens. And bb-blaming fathers… When I was about to dd-die-

ALAN. Excuse me?

OLD MAN. I'm sorry. I thought you wanted to ttt-talk. You looked like you cc-could use a little chat.

ALAN. No, it's just what you said. When I was about to die-

KATE. I'm glad he met your brother, please don't misunderstand me. It has given him strength through all my… Oh dear God- If I am seeing you, does that mean?

SARAH. Do your hands still hurt?

KATE Yes, look at them. The nails are turning brown. From the chemo.

SARAH. When our bellies were aching from hunger, my mother used to say to hold on to that ache because it means that you are still alive.

OLD MAN. Yes, well I don't know why I should have been so shocked. I was 120. Not exactly a sss-spring chicken as they say…Bbb-but the Lord wanted to take me. He appeared before me –

ALAN. Wait- Wait. Let me wrap my brain around this one. People play this game if you could have a conversation with just one person in history…and alright, I can't lie and say you were first or second on my list- but you certainly made the top ten. I have so many questions I promised I would ask you. Okay, first, what did he look like?

OLD MAN. The Lord? You mean burning bb-bush or long white b-bbeard?

ALAN. Yes. I mean, look at you. You look nothing like-

OLD MAN. Charlton Heston?

ALAN. Yes.

OLD MAN. I know. I bb-begged them for Spencer Ttt-Tracey…This is a very difficult question to answer, but the bbb-best that I can ppp-ut it is close your eyes and think. How does God look to you. Well, that is exactly what appeared before me. And I was atop the mountain watching my people cross into our land, and God appeared and said that it was ttt-time. I had served long and well. But I was not ready, and so I argued- I dddid that a lot- The Lord brought out the tt-tiger in me. And it is in our nature to haggle- I said- "for one hundred twenty years I have done your bidding and served you well have I not?" Notice I never ssss-stammered with the Lord. DDD-duh! "So why must I die? Adam, he disobeyed you. Abraham and Isaac doubted you." And the Lord said "Prepare yourself." But I cried out: "I alone have served you faithfully. Why can I not live forever?" And very simply, no thunder or lightening this time, almost as if in despair, the Lord said: "Did I ask you to kill that Egyptian all those years ago. With your own hands?" And the rest, as they say, is hhh-history.

KATE. I am so tired. I just don't know if it is worth the struggle. I am so tired of fighting the fight.

SARAH. May I tell you a story? I talk about it in my lectures, about Israel, but perhaps it will help. It helped me. *(Kate reaches out to touch her to say yes. Her hand is resting on one side of the glass. SARAH. touches the other. There is only the thickness of glass between them)* There was once a man whose only son had a great gift for painting. People paid a hundred zloty for

94

a single one of his paintings. One day he told his father he was going out beyond the city to where there was a tall tower on a high hill. The father did not want this and tried to convince his son not to go. But he could not dissuade him, so the man followed his son. It took them a long time to reach their destination and climb the tower, but once they did, the son began to paint a picture of the most glorious view and lush green hill. After several weeks, the painting was finished. When the artist looked at the right side from a distance, he did not find the painting pleasing. The farther back he stood from the right side the uglier the painting was to him. The thought occurred to him: begin over again, from the very beginning. But no! He reconsidered and decided to look at the reverse side of the painting. The farther he stood back from it, the more beautiful the picture appeared to him. And each step further back he stood, the more beautiful it seemed. As he watched his son move farther and farther backwards, the father suddenly realized his son was in great danger. One additional step and he would plunge from the tower. So the father seized the paintbrush and smeared paint across the picture, ruining it. The son rushed towards his father crying: "Father, what have you done? I worked so hard on this. I put everything, my heart and soul into this work, and now you have destroyed it." "Yes, I know," the father said "but now you will live to paint again. And you will paint so many more beautiful and splendid pictures." *(They pull their hands back and there are only handprints now on the glass.)*

> *Jacob rushes into the waiting room and Alan is alone, asleep with the Time magazine and the notebook of Sarah's writings on his lap.*

JACOB. Alan, forgive me for coming so late. I got lost. I thought I was uptown but it was down.

ALAN. That's all right, my friend. Thank you so much for coming.

JACOB. How is she doing? Where is everybody? I thought the cast would be here…

ALAN. I asked them to leave. I wanted to be alone for awhile. *(Refers to the magazine)* Did you see this, Jacob? The suicide bombing de jour was a woman. Walked into a café and blew herself up. For the first time a young woman.  How bad is it when woman are willing to die like this for their cause… How will it ever be stopped now? And she was a nurse, a paramedic… My wife wants nothing more than to live and across the world some other woman wants to blow herself to bits, no worse- believes it is the honorable thing, a holy thing to piss her life away and any others-- for her cause, for her beliefs…This is what faith gets you. Kate is inoperable, Jacob. The doctor used that word for the first time. What a horrible sounding thing… How can a word carry so much fear… apparently if they had gone

ahead and cut out her lung, it wouldn't have done any good. There is a spread to the other lung so… They have to continue chemo. They kept reassuring us not to give up hope, that remission is still very possibl, but that we need to look at this as a manageable disease, like asthma or HIV; there's a comforting thought…Cancer can be managed…It can be suppressed, something one just lives with…Sounds to me awful like the occupied territories... Put up some fences and learn to live with our cancer…
I was so angry- she woke up in the post-op, and they told her before they let me in to see her, so when I got there she was all alone and crying, sobbing and as I held her, I could feel her shaking, and then she just stopped. And then she looked at the doctor and said- "Okay- that really sucks doesn't it, but so now what are we going to do?"

JACOB. She is so strong. Her faith is like a mountain.

ALAN. It is not faith that is the key, Jacob. Faith is just food. It feeds you, but the key is her will. We will ourselves to live, to achieve, to believe, to do good- Yes, faith is important, so is love, or hope, and sometimes all three- but it is that resolve, that determination, the fricking rock hard fortitude of the human spirit that I am in awe of…

SARAH. Am I alive now, during these fine May days, when beautiful nature is also alive? The birch woods whisper from a distance, the little birds sing their quiet melodic songs of praise and soar in the clean air.

ALAN. I just hope I have the will…You have it- and so did your sister. I've been reading Sarah. She's been a great help.

JACOB. I am glad.

ALAN. Can we go for a walk? They gave Kate a sedative for the pain, so she is sleeping. I'd like to go outside.

SARAH. The little river suns along quietly without any murmuring or any noisy waves. The rested fields are sown. Everything is magnificent, all of nature so full of life and so delightful. Unmoved by our situation, it goes on living, budding, developing, changing color.

ALAN. *(As they move outside)* How did you ever make it, Jacob? How did you ever find the strength?

JACOB. I almost didn't. Do you know that out of the window of the camp at Minsk you could see the Alps. It was like a postcard. Never have you seen such a beautiful sight.

ALAN. Remember how blue the sky was September 11th? Downtown there was carnage, but just blocks away if you looked north, the sky was crystal-clear, and it was a crisp fall day…

JACOB. Those mountains covered in clouds were so cruel…Everyday you saw them but knew they were a lifetime away...

JAKOV. Strength?  Schmength.

JACOB. Some days I would have welcomed death. Especially after I lost my Taté.

DAVID. You must never say that, Yankele. You must always tell yourself to live. We need each other, don't we?

JACOB. He was so sick he could not even stand. I had survived typhus only because he had visited me every day, calling for me through the fence, telling me how much he looked forward to my return. That I must get well. And when I did get stronger, he was so proud of me, but by that time he was ready to go. He was so weak and-

JAKOV. Your feet are so swollen-

DAVID. Yankele, my sweet boy, I could do much more for you if I were closer to God. Your grandfather will be with me. He will take care of me. He'll give me cake and schnapps like he used to… Our plan- it has worked. We survived for this long, now it is your turn. You must forget about me. I will let God take me, but I will not let him rest. I will fight with him and beg him until he promises to let you survive. Now, this is what you must do. It is time for you to escape, to become a Partisan, to fight as you have always wanted to. Hide in the potato cellar and when it gets dark, run for the forest. Do not worry. God is on both sides of the fence.

JACOB. But when I tried to escape, I saw Rontshka was there. Two others had been caught, and we were all made to watch their immediate execution. And the next day, again we were loaded onto trains. By now Father could no longer speak. For the first time there was no plan…They had to carry him off the transport and into Mauthausen, and they started to take him away from us with the sick and dying, and I remember screaming: "He needs me. He needs me. My Taté, he needs me." But a guard hit me with a rifle, and said, "He needs you no more."

SARAH. Do I live or am I already dead? Am I in a dark wood and dreaming such things, or in a place laid to waste where there are only sky and hot sand. Or perhaps in some world of the dead, or among demons perhaps?

JACOB. There was no food in Mauthausen, but I did not care. I ate a piece of coal that I found- it tasted bitter, but not bad… Later a doctor told me it may have saved me from the dysentery. Some of the others were eating the dead… I do remember that…

SARAH. Leave me, you thoughts that I do not want to consider. Go away and let me live in peace and quiet, free of torment. In my final moments, let me depart quietly from this beautiful world. I wish to be left alone and quiet.

*The ensemble is lying on the floor of the stage now.*

JACOB. I never stood again after that, I, too, had become weak. My feet were twice the size. We were lying there; I could feel the others, heard the gasps, the moans, but little else.

SARAH. Why do you persist in delving deeper and deeper and give me no respite, and why, my thoughts, do you refuse to have compassion for my heart, which no longer beats normally. Perhaps I am writing all of this in a fantastic, ephemeral dream on the day I feel I am about to drop and remain lying there, and I am groaning and weeping in my sleep and no one heeds me.

*From the back of the theater the sound of tanks can be heard, and it should become deafening. They stop and a voice can be heard on a loud-speaker: "Come out. Come outside. You are free. You have been liberated. Come out of your barracks, you are free!" It is raining all over the stage now.*

JACOB. I remember waking, though I do not remember falling asleep, and some of the others, the only few that could move were trying to stand. And the weakest of us said, "If we are meant to die, let us at least die outside in the clean air." And we took each other's arms, there must have been five or six of us, and this five or six had the strength of one, the strength to stumble outside. And then we collapsed into the mud. It was raining, you see. But the ground, the mud, felt so soft and cool; the rain touched our faces, washing over us. And I opened my eyes wide and drank the water. I think of those drops every time I take a drink. I was the only one of those five or six to stand up from that mud. The others died right then and there, but they died in the fresh air, cleansed by the rain.

*Jacob hands Alan the diary in a simple plastic bag.*

ALAN. Why are you giving me this?

JACOB. I am not giving it to you. I am giving it to your school. It belongs there. With the students. You must build a place for it. Sarah would be so happy, so proud. She can be with students from all over, and they can hear her stories.

ALAN. I will. I will try.

JACOB. You'd better. This God of ours does have a temper… I don't mean to nudge, but do you have any idea when this play of yours might be finished?

ALAN. It may be finished. I'm close. I'll let you know.

JACOB. Good because none of us are getting any younger, you know.

SARAH. Why can't we live a normal life, achieve our goals, and then approach our seventies, not yet having suffered death from natural causes? Yes, I am writing! Am I still alive? Is it my living thoughts that are dictating to me, and are these, in truth, my final moments? I am still writing as I think: Who knows where the pages of my beloved diary will be blowing tomorrow? Where, my dear pages, will the harsh wind scatter you, driving you far away from her who loves you? Who will guard and treasure you as I do? Thou didst deliver us from Egypt. I end my confession and still retain the hope that perhaps by Thy Will and Thy Leave all of us may go on living.

JACOB. Come on, let us get out of the rain and see this wife of yours. She will be awake soon, no? Where did we come from? I get so lost…You lead the way…
    *They get up and leave, and as the lights fade, Jakov is seen writing.*

ENSEMBLE. **Denver Colorado, America. The 5th of June, 1950.**

JAKOV. My hands tremble, and I am dizzy as I take my pen in hand and write on this paper, in your diary, where you recorded the days of your life as they passed, where you recorded your joy and your…

*The lights have faded.*

### *End of the Play*